D0897738

## Donated by

*Angela Long*

*In Memory of*

*Jack Bowser*

# TALES FROM THE
# PITTSBURGH PIRATES
# DUGOUT

## A COLLECTION OF THE GREATEST PIRATES STORIES EVER TOLD

## JOHN McCOLLISTER

SPORTS
PUBLISHING

*Dedicated to:*

*My beautiful bride, Sarah, my beloved*
*partner in life and a fanatic fan*
*of the Pittsburgh Pirates*

Sports Publishing books may be purchased in bulk at special discounts for sales promotion, corporate gifts, fund-raising, or educational purposes. Special editions can also be created to specifications. For details, contact the Special Sales Department, Sports Publishing, 307 West 36th Street, 11th Floor, New York, NY 10018 or sportspubbooks@skyhorsepublishing.com.

Sports Publishing® is a registered trademark of Skyhorse Publishing, Inc.®, a Delaware corporation.

Visit our website at www.sportspubbooks.com.

10 9 8 7 6 5 4 3 2 1

Library of Congress Cataloging-in-Publication Data is available on file.

ISBN: 978-1-61321-346-9

Printed in the United States of America

# Acknowledgments

No book is ever written in a vacuum. Helping with a project such as this is a crew of experts and friends, without whom writing this volume would have been impossible.

Special thanks goes to Pittsburgh marketing and public relations consultant Todd Miller for his assistance with editing and fact finding, to Scott Rauguth, Noah Amstadter and Bob Snodgrass of Sports Publishing L.L.C., and to Alice Martell the world's greatest literary agent.

Thanks, too, to the family of the Pittsburgh Pirates, especially CEO and managing general partner Kevin McClatchy, director of media relations Jim Trdinich, vice president of marketing and broadcasting Vic Gregovits, manager of media services Dan Hart, photographer David Arrigo, and Hall of Famer Ralph Kiner. Their cooperation and encouragement have been extremely valuable.

Finally, my thanks to the most knowledgeable baseball people in the world—the fans of the Pirates, who are always ready with a fact, a story, and especially an opinion. You have celebrated the triumphs and have endured the disappointments, yet you have never lost your loyalty to the team. The marriage between you and your Pirates is one that will last as long as the city of Pittsburgh exists. You are the best!

# Contents

# Introduction

This is a love story. This is a collection of tales about a lifelong relationship between a baseball team and its fans.

The story of the Pittsburgh Pirates overflows with anecdotes and illustrations that tell us a lot about the team, about the city, and about the people who call Pittsburgh their "home." In a sense, the history of the Pirates is a mirror image of the people who were schooled in the "steel mill mentality."

The citizens of Western Pennsylvania are products of a wide variety of ethnic cultures, religions and traditions. At the same time, the parents and grandparents who formed Pittsburgh's unique cultural mosaic share one common heritage—they have instilled in their sons and daughters a solid work ethic that includes pride in a job well done and the willingness to give an honest day's work for their pay.

At the same time, as some of the tales in this book reveal, they abhor those who think too highly of themselves, or who try to get something for nothing.

That's especially true when Pittsburghers follow the actions, both on and off the field, of those who represent their city while wearing the black and gold of the Pirates. Win or lose, they cheer and support the players who give 100 percent on the field by hustling to first on a routine ground ball, and they vent their disappointment on those who approach the game with a nonchalant attitude.

The team has been blessed over the past 100-plus years with a colorful cast of characters who have never been shy about revealing their true feelings on a subject. Like their fans, these players also hail from a variety of racial, ethnic and geographic backgrounds, but find a common focus in never giving up until the last out is recorded. Likewise, Greater Pittsburgh, with its multitude of boroughs, townships and districts, becomes united when its citizens pass through the turnstiles at PNC Park and prepare to cheer for their Buccos.

Like the Pirates players, the residents of Pittsburgh work hard, play hard, even fight hard—sometimes among themselves. However, once the battles have been waged and tempers wane, they put the past behind them and head for the nearest watering hole to share a cool Iron City Beer.

In writing this book, the author selected representatives of the Pirates who share interesting stories. Some of them will make you laugh; some could bring a tear; others may cause you to shake your head in wonder. Whatever the case, may these tales add a sparkle to your day and enhance your enjoyment of Pittsburgh baseball.

JCM

# Babe Adams

The 1909 World Series pitting the National League champion Pittsburgh Pirates against the American League's Detroit Tigers has provided a rich background for plenty of stories. It featured a head-to-head confrontation between the game's two most trumpeted players—the Pirates' outstanding shortstop Honus Wagner and perhaps the greatest Tiger ever, Tyrus Raymond Cobb.

During the Series, Wagner clearly out-dueled Cobb in nearly every offensive department. But the unsung hero of the seven-game Series was a shy 27-year-old from Tipton, Indiana, Charles "Babe" Adams. In this, his first full year in the majors, the baby-faced (hence his nickname) right-hander compiled an impressive 12-3 record with a 1.11 earned run average to match. But it was in this 1909 World Series that his star began to shine.

Adams scattered six hits as he and the Bucs won the opening game in Pittsburgh by a score of 4-1. He pitched and won Game 5 by an 8-4 margin. And, if there was any question as to who should be world champions, Adams put an exclamation mark on the answer when he shut out the Tigers, 8-0, in Game 7.

No pitcher before had ever won three games in a best-of-seven World Series.

That evening, Pittsburgh fans celebrated up and down Smithfield Street. For the first time in history, their Pirates were the kings of baseball.

*Charles "Babe" Adams won three of the four victories for the Bucs in the 1909 World Series.*

# Pedro Alvarez

Not since the eras dominated by sluggers Ralph Kiner, Willie Stargell, Dick Stuart, and (for a brief time) Dino Restelli have the Pirates sent to the plate a home-run threat such as Pedro Alvarez. This 6', 3", 235-pound left hand powerhouse, a native of Santa Domingo, has sometimes frustrated the Pirate faithful with his high percentage of strikeouts; at the same time he has thrilled fans with his towering home runs—some of which have flown over the right-field stands at PNC Park only to be baptized into the Monongahela River more than 450 feet from home plate.

Anticipating that he was on the threshold of a breakout season, Pirate brass were not excited in January 2010 when, shortly before the start of spring training, they learned that 23-year-old Alvarez had added an additional 15 pounds to his frame.

His excuse was that, over the winter, he had taken a substantial break from his normal training routine in order to marry his fiancé—a marathon runner.

While the challenge of losing 15 pounds may not be a monumental task for a person of his age, Pirate management expressed more than a little concern about his added poundage. "After all, we don't want our third baseman to prepare to be a candidate for Pittsburgh's version of a sumo wrestler," noted one executive.

Pedro's excuse for his added girth was simple. "Guess I just ate too much wedding cake."

Eventually he was able to shed the unwanted pounds and, today, remains one of the premier long-ball hitters in all of baseball.

# Harold Arlin

On August 5, 1921, the Pittsburgh Pirates won a game against Philadelphia by a score of 8-5. But it wasn't the score that was significant. Instead, it was the fact that the Pirates that afternoon began a practice that has been copied by every big-league club since. As an "experiment," the Pirates, in cooperation with KDKA radio, broadcast the first game ever for a team in Major League Baseball.

Announcing that memorable game was 26-year-old Harold Arlin, who confessed years later that the success of the broadcasts came as a complete surprise to him and his bosses. "Our broadcast—back then, at least—wasn't that big a deal. Our guys at KDKA didn't even think that baseball would last on radio. I did it as a one-shot project."

Since there were no such facilities as a broadcast booth at the ballpark, Arlin fulfilled his assignment while sitting in a box seat at Forbes Field.

\* \* \*

Before Harold Arlin broadcast that first Major League Baseball game on radio, owner Barney Dreyfuss and the rest of Pirates management were skeptical about airing a play-by-play description of the games. They feared fans would opt to listen to the games on their Zenith consoles instead of taking the time to ride streetcars to Schenley Park and fight the crowds for a decent seat at Forbes Field.

To the pleasant surprise of the Pirates' brass, just the opposite happened. Radio broadcasts created a wider interest. New fans—women, in particular—learned about the game and became familiar with players' names. They flocked to Forbes Field to see for themselves the players about whom they had only heard. As a result, during 1921, a total of 701,567 fans passed through the turnstiles—an increase of nearly 300,000 from the year before.

# Clyde Barnhart

Third baseman/outfielder Clyde "Pooch" Barnhart played for the Bucs during his entire nine-year big-league career (1920-1928). A lifetime .295 hitter, he set a record against the Cincinnati Reds on October 2 in his rookie year that will probably never be equaled. On that one day, the young native of Buck Valley, Pennsylvania, hit safely in three games. It happened during the last *tripleheader* ever played in Major League Baseball.

# Tony Bartirome

If there is one thing that even the most faithful fan of the Pittsburgh Pirates would be willing to forget, it's the 1952 version of the team.

Executive Vice President and General Manager Branch Rickey orchestrated the activities from behind his desk in his executive office suite. Rickey was interested in several things, including enhancing his public image and seeing that the financial records for the ball club showed a bottom-line profit.

One of the items on his agenda was not one that headed the list of most men in his position: producing a winning team. The final standings of that year showing a last-place finish with an anemic record of on 42 wins and a whopping 112 losses was testimony to his determination to eschew any realistic hopes for a World Series championship for the Steel City.

Outside of future Hall-of-Famer Ralph Kiner (who would led the league in home runs [37] that season for a record seventh year in a row), no player on the roster was what you would call a "household name."

Personifying the plight of the team was 19-year-old Tony Bartirome, a slick-fielding first baseman.

Most teams and seasoned baseball observers consider first basemen to be heavy-hitters who are destined to give pitchers and other opposing members an abundance of fear as to what might happen were he to connect on a hard swing.

Unfortunately for Pirates fans everywhere, Tony Bartirome was not blessed with such gifts. Instead, during his only big-league season, he batted a mere .220 with a total of 16 runs batted in and 0 home runs.

His only noteworthy statistic from the batter's box was the fact that during the 124 games in which he appeared during that ill-fated season, Tony Bartirome did not once hit into a double play.

Someone might ask why it is that a regular member of the squad who came to bat 355 times in the National League that year could accomplish that record. Today, Tony, who lives in Bradenton, Florida, offers a logical explanation: "I simply never hit the ball hard enough to allow the opposition to complete a short-to-second-to-first double killing."

Following his one-year tenure with the Bucs, Tony was drafted into the U.S. Army and served for two years. After his tour of duty he hung up his glove but was invited by the front office to return to the Pirates in 1967, this time as head trainer until 1985. He thus became the only former Major League Baseball player to serve as a club's official trainer. During that period in his life one of his challenges was to keep Roberto Clemente in the lineup through his nagging aches and pains—a major accomplishment, indeed.

# Ted Beard

Speedy outfielder Ted Beard—standing 5'8" and weighing 165 pounds—played for the Pirates from 1948-1952. During that time, he batted .198 and hit a grand total of five home runs. In short, he was not exactly a powerhouse with a bat. But on July 16, 1950, against Boston Braves pitcher Bob Hall, the left-hander did something that would amaze the likes of illusionist David Copperfield. He swung hard at an inside fastball and sent it soaring high and deep to right field. Both Beard and the Braves players watched in utter amazement as the ball continued to sail over the roof of the 86-foot-high grandstand. Ted Beard became the first player ever to hit a ball over the right-field roof at Forbes Field since Babe Ruth accomplished that feat for the first time 15 years earlier.

One of the eyewitnesses in the Pirates' dugout that afternoon was reserve catcher Ray Mueller who, ironically, was a rookie for the Braves in 1935 and had also seen the Babe Ruth clout.

*With one swing, Ted Beard equaled the great Babe Ruth with a colossal blast in 1950.*

# Bensy Benswanger

On April 9, 1934, a cold, blustery Sunday afternoon, the Pirates defeated the Cincinnati Reds by a score of 9-5. Making headlines the next day was not the outcome of the game. It was the fact that the game was played on a Sunday.

When Pittsburgh fielded a major-league team in 1882, conservative Christian groups, combined with the so-called Pennsylvania "Blue Laws," pressured the club into refraining from playing its games on Sunday "lest we violate the Lord's Sabbath." That tradition continued until William "Bensy" Benswanger, son-in-law of the late Barney Dreyfuss and the man who succeeded Mr. Dreyfuss as owner of the Pittsburgh Baseball Club, learned how other teams had profited from tickets sold for Sunday games. He was not about to let such a golden opportunity slip from his grasp.

Through persistent negotiations and constant references to the dwindling finances in the municipal treasury, Benswanger was able to persuade the city fathers that the additional revenue would be in the best interest of the fair citizens of Pittsburgh. Games, therefore, were permitted at Forbes Field on two conditions: management would allow no beer to be sold at the ballpark on Sundays and it would allow no inning of a Sunday baseball game to begin after 7:00 p.m. This would allow fans enough time to leave the park and attend evening church services. These practices remained in effect at Forbes Field until the early '50s.

* * *

By September 1, 1938, the Pirates were well on their way to capturing the National League pennant. After winning 40 out of 54 games in June and July, the Bucs grabbed a commanding seven-game lead over Chicago and Cincinnati, who were tied for second. But during September, the Cubs began to flex their muscles and inched their way closer to the Pirates.

During the Pirates' late-season swing through Philadelphia and Brooklyn, a hurricane lashed its force against the Eastern seaboard. By the time the winds died down and conditions became playable, the Bucs had lost the opportunity to play four games against the last-place Phillies and seventh-place Dodgers. Rainouts were not made up during this era. Meanwhile, the Cubs kept winning.

The final blow to Pittsburgh's quest for a National League title was a three-game series with the Cubs during the last week of the season. The Bucs, who had come to Wrigley Field with a lead of three and a half games, lost all three contests, including one game that featured the legendary "Homer in the Gloamin'" hit by Cubs player/manager Gabby Hartnett. Eventually the Cubs won the pennant by two and a half games.

Owner Benswanger, to his dying day, blamed the Pirates' demise on the hurricane. "The pennant," he said, "was lost *before* the Cubs series. The hurricane prevented us from winning. To lose a pennant by losing ball games is one thing; to lose by idleness is another."

* * *

Ben Benswanger and the others in the Pirates' front office were so convinced that their team would run away with the National League pennant in 1938, they constructed a third tier of seats approximately eight feet below the overhanging roof of the grandstands in Forbes Field to accommodate the anticipated hordes of reporters from the national media who would descend upon Pittsburgh for the Fall Classic.

Alas, those new seats, as well as the rest of the ballpark, remained empty during the World Series, as the National League champion Chicago Cubs were losing four straight games to Joe DiMaggio and the New York Yankees.

Until Forbes Field was demolished in 1971, the seats remained—each one a testimony to over-confidence.

# Louis Bierbauer

Baseball squabbles between owners and players over salaries are not new. In 1889, players who sought more money for their talents bolted from their existing teams in order to form a new league aptly called the "Players League." It folded after only one year. When the league disbanded, the players were forgiven for their past decisions to leave if they returned to the clubs they had left the year before.

One of those players was Louis Bierbauer, a second baseman with solid, albeit unglamorous, credentials for the Philadelphia Athletics of the American Association (a forerunner of the American League). Through a clerical mix-up, Bierbauer's name did not appear on the list of players eligible to return to his former team. J. Palmer O'Neill, president of the Pittsburgh Baseball Club, quickly noted the error and offered Bierbauer a contract. Bierbauer accepted.

The American Association protested, and the matter went to arbitration. The arbitrator ruled in favor of Pittsburgh. A spokesman for the American Association exclaimed, "The action of the Pittsburgh Club is piratical!" J. Palmer O'Neill soon became "J. *Pirate* O'Neill" in the newspapers.

The less-than-flattering nickname stuck. From that time forward, the official team name for Pittsburgh would no longer be the "Alleghenies" (their designation ever since being founded in 1882), but the "Pirates."

Today, at PNC Park, the Pirates' home since 2001, one of the restaurants is called "Bierbauer's" to recognize the significance of that name in team history.

# Steve Blass

Formerly a Pirates star and now a popular radio and television announcer, Steve Blass is the subject of one of baseball's most famous unsolved mysteries.

Blass was a major factor in the Pirates' race for the pennant and ultimate World Series championship in 1971. With a record of 15-8 and a league-leading five shutouts that year, and 19-8 in '72, Blass dazzled opposing batters with his patented "slop drop" pitch and pinpoint control.

For some unexplained reason, in 1973, Steve Blass couldn't find home plate with a compass. He still possessed the physical attributes of a solid pitcher; he just could not throw strikes. He ran through a gauntlet of professionals—doctors, coaches, hypnotists, psychologists and psychiatrists—in search of an explanation. Nothing worked.

Blass pitched only 89 innings that year (compared to the 250 he tossed a year earlier) and gave up 84 walks (the same number he issued in all of '72). He posted a 3-9 record, and his ERA mushroomed from 2.49 to a whopping 9.81. He retired from baseball the next year after pitching only five innings.

To this day, complete strangers approach him on the street and ask, "What happened to you in. . . ?" Before they have a chance to finish the question, Blass shrugs his shoulders and answers, "Frankly, I don't know. I wish I did."

\* \* \*

A sudden lack of control by Steve Blass in 1973 was rather amazing, since the right-hander had clearly established himself as one of baseball's most accurate pitchers. His longtime catcher, Manny Sanguillen, claimed the 31-year-old native of Canaan, Connecticut, could divide home plate into thirds. "That made my job much easier," said Sanguillen. "Both of us knew exactly where the ball would be pitched. He was so precise, I felt I could catch Steve Blass while sitting in a rocking chair."

\* \* \*

Steve Blass has become a near legend today because of his sudden inability to find a strike zone in '73. A story was passed around the nation via the Associated Press about a time during the 2002 season in Cincinnati when Blass was broadcasting a Pirates game and happened to catch a foul ball hit back into the television booth. According to the report, Blass attempted to drop the ball to a youngster in the stands. Instead, the ball hit a man on the head, bounced and hit another kid on the head. Steve Blass commented, "See, I still don't have any control."

\* \* \*

The final game of the 1972 National League Championship Series (NCLS) is one that the Pirates would probably rather forget. Going into the best-of-five series against Cincinnati, the Pirates were heavy favorites. Not only were they the defending world champions, they packed their lineup with some heavy artillery, including Roberto Clemente, Willie Stargell, Manny Sanguillen, Richie Hebner, Bob Robertson and Al Oliver. In addition, the pitching staff of Steve Blass, Nellie Briles, Dock Ellis, Bruce Ki-

*A mysterious fate greeted Pirate star pitcher (now announcer) Steve Blass in 1973.*

son, Dave Giusti and Bob Moose could match that of any squad in either league.

Cincinnati did not raise a white flag in surrender, however. They clawed and scrapped their way to tie the series at two games apiece.

In the deciding game at Cincinnati's Riverfront Stadium on October 11, behind the pitching of Steve Blass (19-8 that year and already a winner in Game 1), the Bucs forged ahead 2-0 on hits by Sanguillen, Hebner and Dave Cash. After the Reds scored a run, the same trio hit safely to put the Pirates ahead, 3-1.

With one out in the bottom of the eighth, and the Bucs still leading, 3-2, manager Bill Virdon called on Ramon Hernandez to relieve Blass. Hernandez finished the inning without allowing a run.

The Pirates still led 3-2 going into the bottom of the ninth. Virdon elected to go with reliever Dave Giusti, who had amassed 22 saves that year. The strategy backfired when the first batter Giusti faced, Johnny Bench, hit a game-tying home run into the right-field stands. What followed became a Pittsburgh nightmare.

Giusti gave up singles to Tony Perez and Dennis Menke. Virdon called for Bob Moose to relieve Giusti. Moose got Cesar Geronimo to fly out, and Perez took third. When Darrel Chaney popped out to short, it looked as though the game would go to extra innings. That was not to happen. Moose got a one-and-one count on pinch hitter Hal McRae when he let go of a sharp slider that broke low and wide. It skipped by catcher Manny Sanguillen toward the backstop, and Perez easily scored the winning run.

A sad, frustrated and angry Pirates team flew back to Pittsburgh. Nobody spoke during the entire flight. The team the experts had picked to repeat as World Series champions now faced a long, cold winter.

Since both families lived in the same section of town, Steve Blass, Dave Giusti and their wives rode from the airport in the same car to their homes. The stone-cold silence continued during the ride. When the car stopped for a traffic light, Blass broke the tension by yelling, "Okay, everybody out for our fire drill! It's time to loosen up."

All four occupants immediately climbed out of the vehicle. "We were so pissed off," recalls Blass, "we started to shout obscenities into the dark of the night. When we got done, we all felt better. We got back into the car and continued our drive home. We were now able to face the winter."

As a postscript to this story, that horrible game of the 1972 NLCS was the last ever played by Roberto Clemente, who was killed in a plane crash the following New Year's Eve.

# Barry Bonds

Barry Lamar Bonds, who played left field for the Pirates from 1986 to 1992, was placed on the ballot for election to Baseball's Hall of Fame for the first time in December 2012.

He did not make it to enshrinement in the hall of heroes that year, having been named on just 36.2 percent of ballots submitted by the Baseball Writers' Association of America. Many speculate that, in all probability, he will never receive the required 75 percent of the votes.

At first glance, a reader might wonder why this mighty slugger would be excluded from consideration for induction. He certainly racked up a resume of solid statistics.

He had the genes (the son of Bobby Bonds and the cousin of Reggie Jackson) to give him a head start for stardom in Major League Baseball. Most amazing, however, were the statistics he racked up over 22 seasons in "The Show." His eye-popping records include being named 14 years as an All Star, 7 years as the National League's Most Valuable Player, and 12 Silver Slugger Awards. In addition, while playing for the San Francisco Giants, during the 2001 campaign he socked an incredible 73 home runs, thus surpassing the feats of immortals of the game such as Babe Ruth and Hank Aaron.

To illustrate the enormous respect for his hitting prowess, on

*Young Barry Bonds swung a potent bat for the Bucs from 1986 through 1992, although his arm was not quite strong enough in the final game of the '92 NLCS.*

several occasions opposing pitchers elected to issue an intentional walk to Bonds *with the bases loaded.*

As to his rejection by the BBWA for enshrinment into the Hall of Fame, Bonds remains puzzled. In a 2012 interview with the *Los Angeles Times* Bonds was quoted as saying, "I don't know how to explain it. The world has become so negative. One day I'll be able to say things the right way. But it's tough when you have so many people out there who don't want to turn the page and want to be angry with you forever. I don't understand why it continues on. What am I doing wrong?"

Anybody who follows baseball would be able to answer that question with one word: Steroids.

From all accounts, Bonds was not on steroids prior to his departure from the Pittsburgh club. Reliable reports maintain that his steroid use began after the hectic year of 1998 when Sammy Sosa of the Cubs and Mark McGwire of the Cardinals were making headlines as a result of a torrid contest for the home run championship. McGwire won the title with 70 round-trippers and Sosa hammered a total of 66. Rumors floated around all of baseball that both sluggers, however, were "juiced"—i.e. on steroids.

Bonds knew he was a better hitter that either of these two. He claimed to have better hand-and-eye coordination. He, therefore, alledgedly yielded to the temptation of fighting fire with fire. He was said to have received regular doses of steroids and testosterone—a clear violation of the rules of baseball.

Pirate fans could see this happening long before others. Compared to Bonds' first seven years in the Majors, they saw his body noticeably swell and his hat size increase measurably.

Bonds' problems escalated over the years. On November 15, 2007, a federal grand jury returned an indictment against the former Buc's left fielder for perjury and obstruction of justice.

In addition, evidence unsealed by the government showed that Bonds had, indeed, used performance-enhacing substances.

Bonds, to this day, continues to proclaim his innocence of all charges against him. He maintains that he never knowingly used steroids.

The drug tests and public opinion seem to disagree with him. Perhaps the saddest thing about this is the opinion held by the majority of baseball experts: based on his records established while he was with the Pirates, without the benefit of steroids, Barry Bonds could have had it all—even induction into the Hall of Fame.

# Everitt Booe

Joining the Pirates in 1913 was a rookie outfielder named Everitt Little Booe. His last name was pronounced with a silent "e," sounding like the common exclamation for Halloween: "Boo!"

Booe's first trip to the plate in a big-league uniform was during spring training as a pinch hitter. Before the young man left the dugout, manager Fred Clarke reminded him to announce his name to the home plate umpire and future Hall of Famer, Bill Klem. Spring training ballparks in those days were not equipped with public address systems, so umpires had to shout out to the opponent's dugout and to the fans the name of any new player entering the contest.

The rookie, eager to make a good impression, grabbed a bat and ran toward the batter's box and stood behind Umpire Klem, who was bent over, dusting off the plate with the customary Wisk broom.

"Booe!" exclaimed the rookie.

Klem stopped sweeping, turned his head and looked up over his shoulder with scowl on his face. "What did you say, kid?"

"Booe!" replied the rookie, this time a bit louder. "I said, Booe!"

"Listen, kid," screamed Klem who now stood nose to nose with the nervous player. "This ain't no joke. If you try to make a fool outta me one more time, I'm gonna kick your ass outta this damn game." Saliva mixed with tobacco juice spewed from the arbiter's mouth as his voice increased in volume. "Ya got that straight? Now, very slowly, just tell me yer name!"

The puzzled rookie was beside himself. Thinking that the veteran umpire may have lost some of his hearing, he stepped back, took a deep breath, and shouted at the top of his lungs, "BOOE!" For emphasis, he repeated his name. "BOOE!"

"Okay, kid, you asked for it. Yer outta here," Klem growled as he pointed straight to the Pirate bench.

Seeing what was happening, Manager Clarke and star out-fielder Max Carey ran from the dugout to the home plate area and explained to Klem the reason for the misunderstanding.

Klem listened patiently, then agreed to permit the youngster to bat. But before he resumed his position behind the plate, Klem paused, looked squarely into the eyes of the now relieved rookie and said, "Kid, if you ever expect to stay in this league, you better change yer *^$*#@$ name."

# Greg Brown

Pirates announcer Greg Brown got his initial on-air experience during the five years he was the play-by-play voice for the Buffalo Bisons minor-league baseball team and as a color analyst and pre- and postgame show host for the National Football League's Buffalo Bills. The broadcast booth, however, wasn't his first assignment with the Pirates. His introduction to Pittsburgh baseball was in uniform on the field in 1979 when he interned in the Pirates' promotions department while a student at Point Park College. No, he did not appear in any of the games as a player, coach or manager. He was hired, instead, as the backup Pirate Parrot during the first year the team featured this mischievous mascot.

# Joe L. Brown

One of the most influential executives in Pittsburgh Pirates history was Joe L. Brown, the team's general manager from 1956-1976. Branch Rickey's so-called "five-year plan" to rejuvenate the Bucs had failed miserably. His replacement, Brown, thereby inherited a team that showed absolutely no potential of winning on a consistent basis. But Joe Brown helped change all that. Within five years, through a combination of skill and some good fortune, he transformed the Pirates from doormats to world champions.

This son of actor/comedian Joe E. Brown had been raised in the fast lane of Hollywood, California. Nonetheless, he shifted all of his interest and energy toward serving Pittsburgh, its team and, especially, its fans. His primary goal in life was to bring to the Steel City a team of which everyone could be proud.

That he did. Throughout the '60s and the '70s, he gave Pittsburgh three world championships. During his tenure, even when the Bucs failed to capture the National League flag, they always remained in contention.

After 20 years of grueling negotiations and deal making, Brown retired to the less stressful life in California, but answered the call to return as "interim" general manager for one year when the team floundered in the mid '80s.

Looking back on his career, Brown admits that he was not a perfect general manager. He laments to this day a decision he had to make during his last two years in the Pirates' front office.

Following the 1975 season, Joe Brown took it upon himself to fire the beloved "Voice of the Pirates," Bob Prince. According to Brown, Prince spent a lot of on-air time, especially if a game got out of hand, rambling with stories totally unrelated to the game. He, the management of radio station KDKA (over which all the games were broadcast) and the team's prime sponsor at the time—The Pittsburgh Brewing Company—asked Prince on several occasions to curtail the stories and stick with the play-by-play. When Prince failed to comply, KDKA management decided that a change would be in order. Brown agreed.

The backlash hit like a six-car pile-up on the Smithfield Street Bridge. Fans wrote, called and cussed the Pirates for firing their beloved "Gunner," a nickname that Prince earned for his rapid-fire on-air delivery. The print media, along with some of the on-air personalities from radio and television—including KDKA—openly challenged the decision. Bob Prince was given a parade in downtown Pittsburgh that drew more than 10,000 people.

"There's no doubt about it," says Brown. "It was a colossal mistake to fire Bob Prince."

# John Candelaria

August 9, 1976, was a special day at Three Rivers Stadium. It marked the 500th game played at the six-year-old stadium. The occasion gave fans even more reason to celebrate when young John Candelaria—"The Candy Man" as he was known—pitched a brilliant, 2-0 shutout against the Los Angeles Dodgers on national television while striking out seven and walking only one. Of most importance is the fact that he allowed no hits. Thus he became the first Pirate ever to pitch a no-hit, no-run game in Pittsburgh.

# Max Carey

The Pirates, like every other major-league club, scout players who have been associated with vocations other than baseball. George "Doc" Medich—an Aliquippa, Pennsylvania, native who pitched for the Bucs in 1976—was a medical student. Others have studied law. Many fans, however, never knew that the Pittsburgh club actually got two of its more productive players out of seminaries.

Maximilian Carnarius "Max" Carey, a fiery, switch-hitting outfielder, spent most of his 20-year major-league career (1910-1929) with the Pirates. He was a terrific player and extremely valuable to the team—leading the National League 10 times in stolen bases and batting over .300 in six seasons with the Bucs, including a career-high .343 during Pittsburgh's successful quest for a world championship in 1925. It looked as though this future Hall of Famer would be a permanent fixture with the Pirates until he got into the doghouse of manager Bill McKechnie, who had accused Carey of failing to hustle. Consequently, Carey led a team revolt against his manager. That got him nothing but trouble from Clarke and from team owner Barney Dreyfuss. To nobody's surprise, Carey was abruptly removed from the Pirates' roster in midseason of 1926 and shipped off to the Brooklyn Dodgers.

Carey did not show these rebellious traits when he was a student at Concordia Lutheran College and Seminary in St. Louis. He was in the second year of a seven-year academic journey to become a candidate for ordination. He received the blessing from his church and from his instructors to pursue his goal to serve as a parish pastor. Carey, however, felt a stronger call—this one to play baseball. He announced his decision to the press in the same simple, unmistakable language he was taught to use while preaching: "I came to the realization that baseball, rather than the holy ministry, was to be my life's work."

All Pittsburgh Pirate fans (with the possible exception of manager Bill McKechnie) sang a *Te Deum* at Sunday church services for this decision.

Following his playing days in the majors, Carey accepted a job in 1943 to assist in the newly formed All-American Girls Professional Baseball League—created to fill the gap left by disbanded minor leagues during World War II. Carey managed the Milwaukee Chicks and the Fort Wayne Daisies. The AAGPBL has been made popular in recent years by the movie *A League of Their Own*.

The other player who traded liturgical vestments for a baseball uniform was Frank Thomas—a slugging outfielder/third baseman who became the team leader in home runs with the departure in 1953 of Ralph Kiner. Thomas, a three-time All-Star selection ('54, '55, '58), who played 16 years in the majors and clouted 286 home runs, studied for the priesthood at Mt. Carmel College in Niagara Falls, Ontario.

Leaving the seminary was a struggle for this Pittsburgh native. But, as he said, "I concluded that my calling was not to spend my professional life in front of an altar, but in front of baseball fans."

# Fred Clarke

Pittsburgh manager Fred Clarke gave owner Barney Dreyfuss fits during the early years of the ball club. Dreyfuss was a dignified businessman who was seldom seen in public without a suit and tie. The docile decorum of this 5'7" German-born banker personified that of a cultured gentleman. Clarke, on the other hand, would look sloppy in a new tuxedo. He was a model of the scrappy, "dirty shirt ballplayer" who refused to back down from anyone.

During one Sunday game in Chicago during the 1900 season, Clarke slid hard into Cubs second baseman Clarence "Cupid" Childs in an attempt to break up a potential double play.

"Do that one more time, and I'll punch you right in the nose," yelled Childs, who avoided getting spiked with a last-second leap into the air.

To Clarke, that wasn't a threat; it was a challenge. Three innings later, Clarke was again on first. At the crack of the bat he again slid, spikes high, into second base. "Immediately," recalled Clarke, "Childs punched me. Naturally, I hit back. Soon we were in a bench-clearing brawl."

Both the Chicago and Pittsburgh newspapers reported the incident in explicit detail. Local reporters, naturally, sided with their hometown heroes. The next day, the two teams were scheduled to play at Exposition Park in Pittsburgh. The papers suggested that Clarke and Childs would finish their fight on the field.

Barney Dreyfuss would have none of this. He called Clarke into his office that Monday morning. "Fred," he said, "I'm tired of your rowdy tactics. If you don't cut them out, I'll have to get rid of you."

Clark responded, "Mr. Dreyfuss, what's the average attendance for a Monday game?"

Dreyfuss checked his ledger. "About 2,200," he said.

That afternoon, the Pirates won the game in a rout, but, contrary to all the newspaper hype, nothing else happened.

The next day, Clarke asked his boss, "Mr. Dreyfuss, how many fans attended yesterday's game?"

"Ah . . . a bit more than 7,200," said Dreyfuss.

Clarke playfully grabbed the owner by his arm. "Barney," he said, "those rowdy tactics are just going to ruin you."

\* \* \*

Player/manager Fred Clarke did everything he could to gain an advantage in a ballgame as the Pirates scrapped for their third National League title in 1903. Clarke fought hard and cussed hard. His favorite targets were umpires.

One particularly close game overflowed with marginal calls. Clarke, contrary to past practice, bit his tongue throughout the afternoon. When first-year arbiter James "Bug" Holliday failed to see the opposing catcher drop a ball and called a Pirates runner out at the plate, Clarke could take it no more. He ran from the bench and unleashed a blistering verbal attack on the rookie umpire. After hearing the string of expletives, Holliday gave Clarke the thumb.

Following the game, Holliday confessed, "I knew what he called me must have been some bad names, but only after I went to my hotel room and looked up those words in a dictionary did I know just how bad they really were."

\* \* \*

*Manager Bill McKechnie, left, gives some tips to a young Fred Clarke.*

Pirates manager Fred Clarke and owner Barney Dreyfuss represented different lifestyles, yet they each shared a mutual respect for the job the other had to do. Clarke respected the fact that Dreyfuss signed the checks and ultimately cast the deciding vote on how the organization should operate. Dreyfuss, too, was keenly aware of the sharp division of responsibility.

Once, following a disappointing loss brought on, in part, by some ragged team play, Dreyfuss burst into the Pirate locker room and demanded to know why the players had not given their all.

Clarke, although angry with his players, directed his wrath against his boss.

"Get out of here and stay out!" he demanded.

Dreyfuss was aghast. "You mean I can't come into my own clubhouse?" he asked.

"Exactly!" said Clarke. "Anytime you want to find fault with the team, you talk to me in private. I'll take the blame. As far as these players, if there is criticism, they'll hear plenty from me, and me alone."

Dreyfuss could have continued the exchange, but he knew Clarke was right. He never again set foot in the locker room without a direct invitation from his manager.

# Roberto Clemente

Thirty-eight-year-old Frank Noah, a native Pittsburgher, was never what one might call a diehard baseball fan. As a youngster he had heard the Pirates games being broadcast by Rosey Rowswell and Bob Prince on WWSW and, later, on KDKA radio. He knew something about the game; however, he never developed a genuine passion for the sport. Frank, in fact, had never seen a Pirates game in person until one evening in 1972 when his Uncle Benny took him to Three Rivers Stadium to watch a contest between the Bucs and the St. Louis Cardinals. They had excellent seats—right behind home plate.

In the top half of the eighth inning, the Pirates were leading by one run. With only one out, Jose Cruz had just tripled for St. Louis and stood on third. The next hitter, Cardinal outfielder Lou Brock, lofted a fly ball to fairly deep right field into the waiting glove of Roberto Clemente. It looked like a routine sacrifice fly that would tie the game.

Cruz tagged up at third and took off for home in a gait somewhat slower than full speed. Big mistake. The large crowd rose to its feet and cheered in anticipation of what was going to happen. Clemente unleashed a cannon-like throw that reached catcher Manny Sanguillen on a fly. Even fans in the cheap seats could see the jovial Sanguillen's bright smile as he held the ball waiting to tag out the unsuspecting Cruz.

Home plate umpire Harry Wendelstedt signaled the runner out, and Pirates fans screamed with delight.

Young Frank, still naïve to the finer points of baseball, turned to his uncle and asked, "Is that normal?"

"No," responded his Uncle Benny. "That was Clemente."

\* \* \*

Veteran Pirates fans still repeat stories about Roberto Clemente's artistry on the diamond. Many of them, however, may not know that his famous number 21, which appears on the facade of the upper deck at PNC Park and set the standard for the height of its right-field wall, was not the number Clemente wore during his rookie season in 1955. That number was 13.

Also, many of the same fans may not know that "Roberto Clemente" wasn't his real name. Instead, in line with the Latin custom of listing one's mother's maiden name second, it was Roberto Clemente Walker. One of the first big-league scouts to see him play was the Dodgers' Al Campanis (the same man who, in 1987, while serving as Dodgers general manager, gained national infamy by unleashing a series of politically incorrect remarks punctuated with racist overtones on Ted Koppel's *Nightline*) had gotten his name mixed up in the translation from Spanish to English during his early days of playing baseball in America, and Clemente did nothing to correct it.

In 2000, the National Baseball Hall of Fame, under the leadership of president Dale Petroskey, spearheaded the replacement of The Great One's original plaque with one that honors the Latin tradition. Visitors to Cooperstown now see a plaque that correctly reads: "Roberto Clemente Walker."

\* \* \*

"I found Clemente in a Dominican tryout camp. He ran the 60-yard dash in 6.4 seconds, and then he threw strikes from center field to home plate. I said to myself, 'If this kid can just hold the bat in his hands, we've gotta sign him.' He hit one line drive after another—even on outside pitches, when that odd swing of his took both of his feet off the ground. He was the greatest amateur athlete I've ever seen. But we lost him, because we gave him a bonus of $10,000 and then failed to protect him in the minor-league draft, and the Pittsburgh scouts swooped in like vultures."

—Al Campanis, former scout and later head of player development for the Brooklyn Dodgers, talking about Roberto Clemente.

* * *

You know you're a great ballplayer when opposing players sing your praises. Tim McCarver, former catcher for the Cardinals, Red Sox and Phillies, described Clemente's ability to throw runners out at the plate: "Some right fielders have rifles for arms, but he had a howitzer."

Hall of Fame pitcher Robin Roberts described Clemente's unorthodox manner of playing the game: "He looked like he was falling apart when he ran. Looked like he was coming apart when he threw. His stance at the plate was ridiculous. When he swung he'd lunge and hit bad balls. There was no way he could hit a ball like that. But no one told Roberto that."

* * *

"Clemente could field a ball in New York and throw a guy out in Pennsylvania."

—Vin Scully, Los Angeles Dodgers Broadcaster

* * *

In 1971, famed writer Roger Angell wrote in *The New Yorker* his interpretation of the play of Roberto Clemente in the World Series that year: "He played the kind of baseball that none of us had ever seen before—throwing and running and hitting at some-

*Willie Stargell greets another Pirate legend,
Roberto Clemente, following a blast out of the park.*

thing close to the level of absolute perfection, playing to win but also playing the game almost as if it were a form of punishment for everyone else on the field."

\* \* \*

"He [Clemente] had the greatest God-given talent I ever saw. There was nothing in the game he couldn't do if he wanted to."
—Dick Groat, Pirates shortstop and team captain.

\* \* \*

Since Roberto Clemente played in a relatively small market, he seldom received accolades from the national press. Following Clemente's stellar performance in the 1971 World Series (still known as "The Clemente Series"), Jerry Izenberg, a writer for *The Star-Ledger* of Newark, New Jersey, wrote: "After 17 major-league seasons, Roberto Clemente is an overnight sensation."

\* \* \*

The late Jim Murray was one of the finest sports reporters who ever punched a keyboard. Readers could always rely upon him for accuracy, yet when it was called for, Murray was never shy about embellishing a fact. After Roberto Clemente displayed such artistry during the '71 World Series, Murray felt that the media and fans expected too much from the talented right fielder. "The thing about Clemente," he once wrote in his column for the *Los Angeles Times*, "is that he's the only guy to receive get-well cards after going five for five, throwing two runners out at the plate, and stealing second standing up."

\* \* \*

In 1968, Paramount Studios filmed the movie version of *The Odd Couple* at New York's Shea Stadium. Part of the script called for a visiting Pittsburgh Pirate to hit into a triple play. The studio offered Clemente $1,000 to do just that in a simulated game. The Great One politely thanked the filmmakers for asking, but passed on the offer. He later explained that the pride he had for himself and for all those he represented would not allow moviegoers to witness him starting a triple play.

The cameo appearance was then given to Bill Mazeroski, who was able to hit a ground ball to the third baseman in just one take.

\* \* \*

Roberto Clemente, Jr., describes his father's warm affection for the Pirates and their city: "My father was born a Pirate. Destiny brought him and the great city of Pittsburgh together."

\* \* \*

Immediately following Roberto Clemente's untimely death in a plane crash on New Year's Eve 1972, tributes throughout the nation poured in. One Pirate fan wrote: "If Roberto Clemente knew how to sing, Harry Belafonte would have to learn to play baseball for a living." Baseball commissioner Bowie Kuhn observed: "He had about him a touch of royalty." Perhaps his epitaph on a memorial plaque in Puerto Rico crystallizes the legend of the man who became known as "The Great One": "I want to be remembered as a ballplayer who gave all he had to give."

\* \* \*

"For me he is the Jackie Robinson of Latin baseball. He lived racism. He was a man who was happy to be not only a Puerto Rican, but also a Latin American. He let people know that. And that is something that is very important for all of us."

—Ozzie Guillen, former major-leaguer.

\* \* \*

On July 25, 1970, the fans in Pittsburgh honored Clemente at a special ceremony prior to a home game. The popular right fielder took this occasion to show how much he appreciated the support of the loyal Pirates fans. He spoke over the Three Rivers Stadium public address system in broken English, but nobody had trouble understanding every word:

"In a way, I was born twice. I was born in 1934, and again in 1955, when I came to Pittsburgh. I am thankful I can say that I live two lives."

# Joe Cronin

Hall of Famer Joe Cronin played in just 50 games as a Pirate during his first two seasons in the majors (1926-1927). He was cut from the squad after appearing in 12 games in '27 while batting a lackluster .227. Still, he was allowed to join his old club in the locker room prior to the first game of the World Series that year against the Yankees at spacious Forbes Field.

The Yankees—with their famed "Murderers Row" that included Babe Ruth (60 home runs), Lou Gehrig (47 home runs), and Tony Lazzeri (18 home runs)—presented a much more potent lineup than did the Pittsburgh team that hit a combined total of 54 homers. In fact, Ruth's total that year exceeded the output of 12 major-league clubs.

Cronin often repeated the story about how the Bronx Bombers put on a hitting exhibition prior to the game that left a psychological impact on the Bucs. In his first trip to the batter's box during batting practice, Ruth asked the pitcher to toss medium-speed fastballs down the middle of the plate, belt-high. Ruth swung and blasted the first pitch deep into the second deck.

Some of the Pirates players who were heading for the clubhouse to change uniforms, heard the ball rattle around the seats. They stopped in their tracks and watched in awe.

Ruth swung again. The ball cleared the 18-foot screen that was added to the nine and a half-foot concrete wall for what would have been another four-bagger.

Ruth drove the next pitch far into the second deck.

Finally, on the fourth pitch, Ruth took a tremendous cut. The ball jumped off the bat and sailed high onto the facade above the right-field stands. By a mere 18 inches, Ruth missed being the first ever to hit a ball completely over that 86-foot-high roof.

Lloyd Waner turned to his brother, Paul, and said, "Jeez. They're big, aren't they?"

Manager Donie Bush whispered to the elder Waner: "Let's go out on the ball field and hope we don't all get killed."

# KiKi Cuyler

One of the most popular center fielders who ever donned a Pirate uniform was Hall of Famer Hazen Shirley "KiKi" Cuyler, who played for the Bucs from 1921-1927. Cuyler, a speed merchant with a potent bat, was a fixture in the third slot of the batting order. During the pennant race in the middle of the 1927 season, the team appeared to demonstrate a lack of enthusiasm for the game—at least in the eyes of its manager, Donie Bush. Adding to the emotional woes for the team was the fact that Cuyler was in the midst of a rare slump.

In an effort to ignite a fire under his players, Bush juggled the lineup and had Cuyler batting second. Cuyler didn't appreciate this. When he went zero for five in his first game while batting second, Cuyler complained to his manager in the clubhouse.

"You'll get used to it," answered Bush.

Cuyler, however, did not. After a particularly poor showing in Cincinnati a few days later, Cuyler demanded, "Take me out of the second slot before I become the worst player on the team."

Bush took this as insubordination. "You'll stay there until I'm ready to change you," he said.

Tension between the two increased and came to a head a few days later when Bush fined Cuyler $25 for failing to slide into second base and break up a double play.

*KiKi Cuyler was a mainstay of the 1927 Pirates, but was benched during the World Series.*

Local sportswriters sided with Cuyler and said so in their columns. The manager viewed this as a conspiracy between Cuyler and the press. In order to show everyone who was in charge, Bush benched the popular Cuyler in favor of a much slower outfielder, Clyde Barnhart.

Fans and the media protested. Bush, however, stood his ground. Cuyler stayed on the bench not only for the rest of the season, but also for the entire World Series, which the Pirates lost in four straight games to Babe Ruth and his New York Yankees.

Many astute baseball historians agree that had Cuyler been permitted to play, the Pirates would not have been shut out in the World Series.

# Brandy Davis

A member of the infamous 1952 Pirates was rookie Robert Brandon "Brandy" Davis—a reserve outfielder with incredible speed. In fact, during one season in the minors, he stole 82 bases in 85 attempts. Unfortunately, he batted only .179 in the 55 games he played for the Pirates that year. Teammate Pete Castiglione said, "If Brandy was allowed to steal first base, he would be a Hall of Famer."

* * *

Former Pirate Joe Garagiola tells the story of when Brandy Davis got his first major-league extra-base hit. In a game against the Cubs at Wrigley Field, when Garagiola was on first with two outs, the right-handed-hitting rookie slammed a line drive to left center field. After the ball bounced off the ivy-covered wall and was thrown back to the infield, Davis was on second with a double, and a winded Garagiola stood huffing and puffing on third. With two outs, the "franchise" for the Pirates that year, Ralph Kiner, strode to the plate.

A lot of fundamental strategies are described in "how to" books on baseball; what happened next is certainly not in any of them. In keeping with the theme set by the '52 Bucs, Davis

*Brandy Davis—if only he could steal first, he would be in the Hall of Fame.*

misread the sign from third base coach Bill Posdell. He thought he got the message to "steal third." No one else, of course, knew what was going through the mind of the rookie.

Perhaps it was due to his confusion while standing on second base (since he had never before seen the diamond from that perspective). For whatever reason, at the instant the pitcher released the ball, Davis darted for third. Garagiola, meanwhile, stood on the bag, looking with sheer amazement at Davis running toward him. Davis slid into the base.

Garagiola raised both hands in the air, showing his disbelief at what he was seeing. "Where are you going?" he screamed.

Without batting an eyelash, Davis looked up and said, "Back to second if I can make it!"

# Johnny Dickshot

Reserve outfielder Johnny Dickshot personified some of the frustration of the 1937 season when the Pirates had fine talent, yet finished the season 10 full games behind the New York Giants. Team owner Bensy Benswanger never knew whether to laugh or cry when he told of one incident. "Dickshot came in for a short fly ball, and when he did so, his cap flew off. Instead of chasing the ball, Johnny chased after his cap, as two runners circled the bases and scored."

# Vince DiMaggio

Two of the famous DiMaggio brothers—Joseph and Dominic—had standout careers in Major League Baseball. A third brother—Vincent—was not quite as successful. The fun-loving Vincent, who spent half of his 10 years in the big leagues playing for the Pirates (1940-1944), was a fair hitter (a lifetime average of .249), yet he often fell victim to the strikeout. In fact, he led the league in whiffs six different times.

His strikeout percentage, however, was not the sole reason Vince DiMaggio left the team. A more devastating gulf between him and Pirates management occurred off the field.

Following a night game in Philadelphia, Vince claimed that the regular dining room at the team's hotel was closed, so he opted to have dinner at Hotel Ben Franklin's swank nightclub. The bill for the repast far exceeded the meal allowance for a player. Sam Watters, the club's treasurer and road secretary, challenged DiMaggio about his check. The challenge soon turned into a shouting match. It proved to be a mighty expensive dinner for Vince. The following winter he was shipped off to the last-place Phillies.

"Now he can eat at Ben Franklin's nightclub much more often," said Watters.

# Ed Doheny

The pressures felt by a Major League Baseball player can be devastating. They certainly got the best of a lovcable Irish pitcher named Edward Doheny. The native New Englander was picked up by Pittsburgh in the middle of the 1901 season. Over a period of two and a half years with the Bucs, the southpaw racked up an impressive 38 wins against only 14 losses.

For some unexplained reason in late July of the 1903 race for the pennant, Doheny developed a "dead arm." Frustration mounted when he could no longer snap off his feared curve ball. In lieu of his customary jovial approach to life, he turned caustic and bitter against his teammates and himself. In the dressing room prior to the last game of the season, when he was told he would not pitch in the first championship series, he clenched his fists and started to swing wildly at anyone within reach.

His teammates quickly subdued him; one of them summoned the police. Within minutes, Doheny was escorted in handcuffs from the locker room and driven to a mental hospital in Danvers, Massachusetts.

Doheny did not respond to treatment, unfortunately. Instead, he physically attacked both a physician and a nurse. He remained a patient at the hospital until his death 13 years later.

# Larry Doughty

Larry Doughty served as general manager for the Pirates during the 1989 season—one of the Bucs' more frustrating years. In spite of the fact that the club fielded a talent-laden team consisting of respected hitters such as Barry Bonds, Andy Van Slyke and Bobby Bonilla, only reserve catcher Mike LaValliere (.316) was able to hit over .300. It's little wonder that the Pirates ended the season in fifth place in the East Division with a 74-88 record, 19 games out of first place.

Commenting on the team's performance, Doughty told a newspaper reporter: "Baseball is supposed to be a non-contact sport, but our hitters seem to be taking that literally."

# Barney Dreyfuss

Pirate owner Barney Dreyfuss began a lot of traditions during his tenure with the club from 1900 until his death in 1932. One of those practices has resulted in millions of fans over the years taking home from ballparks a free souvenir.

In the early days of the sport, the paying customers tossed back onto the field baseballs that were hit into the stands. In one game during the 1921 campaign at Forbes Field, three fans were placed under arrest because they refused to throw back foul balls. A Pittsburgh police officer even wrestled one of the more aggressive fans to the ground. The fan later threatened to sue both the officer and the City of Pittsburgh for damages.

The Pirates agreed to an out-of-court settlement with the demonstrative fan, and on July 9 of that same year, Mr. Dreyfuss, along with Robert J. Allderdice, the City's director of public safety, released the following statement: "Fans who attend games at the National League baseball park here may keep balls knocked into the stands without fear of being molested by policemen."

Thus began a tradition still observed to this day in every Major League Baseball park.

\* \* \*

When his new stadium was built in Pittsburgh, owner Barney Dreyfuss had the distinct honor of selecting the name for the modern structure. Prior to the first game at the new venue, Dreyfuss rifled through more than 100,000 entries submitted by fans in a citywide contest to name the facility.

Dreyfuss chose to name his ballpark not after a famous player or in honor of a famous American. He selected, instead, the name of a British General—John Forbes—who led an expedition against

*Owner Barney Dreyfuss shaped the Pirates in their inaugural seasons.*

the French who had occupied Fort Duquesne located at what is now known as "The Point" where the Allegheny and Mononga-hela Rivers form the Ohio. The fort was destroyed by the French before they fled the scene. It was later rebuilt and renamed Fort Pitt in honor of Sir William Pitt, Prime Minister of Great Britain.

\* \* \*

Barney Dreyfuss's new Forbes Field, built along Forbes Avenue on the site of Schenley Farms, which was used for grazing cattle, was one of the most spacious in all of major-league history. The backstop was 110 feet behind home plate. The left field line reached 360 feet, and the chalk stretched 376 feet in right. Center field was a pitcher's dream; the deepest part was 462 feet from the batter's box—so deep, in fact, that the batting cage used in pregame practice was wheeled up against the center field wall and left there during the game. No player, so said the experts, could ever hit the ball that far.

\* \* \*

Barney Dreyfuss did not allow his Pirates to play home games on a Sunday. He made his decision not as a result of personal religious feelings (Dreyfuss was Jewish) or as a response to pressure from the right-wing Christian community. Instead, he based his choice on how it might affect the bottom line of the treasurer's books. Dreyfuss was soundly convinced that playing ball on a Sunday afternoon "would kill our Saturday afternoon business."

This was one of the rare times Dreyfuss made a serious error in judgment. When Sunday ball eventually was played in Pittsburgh in 1934—two years after Dreyfuss died—attendance at Saturday games actually increased.

\* \* \*

The 1903 championship series (actually, it was the first World Series, but that designation had not yet been given) between the

Pirates and the Boston Pilgrims, was won by the upstart Boston club in a best-of-nine series, five games to three.

Although their team had lost the championship, the Pirates players actually earned more money than did the victors. That was because owner Barney Dreyfuss tossed the entire club owner's share of the receipts into the players' pool. Hence, each Pirate cashed a check for $1,316, whereas each Pilgrim received only $1,182.

# ElRoy Face

Pitcher ElRoy Face spent 16 years in the majors, 15 of them with the Pirates from 1953-1968. During the late 1950s, he developed a new pitch called a "forkball" and, as a result, developed into one of the game's premier relief artists. His best year, without a doubt, was in 1959 when he racked up 18 wins against only one loss.

During that spectacular season, in the midst of all the adulation from the press, an All-Star Game selection and appearances on national television, Face remained undaunted by all the hoopla. One interviewer asked how he could stand all the pressure of entering a situation with the game on the line. Face's response was a classic. "A lot of people have asked me how I can stand the pressure of relief pitching. Well, to me, I don't feel like I have pressure. I have eight guys to help me. The batter has nobody."

\* \* \*

ElRoy Face tied Walter "The Big Train" Johnson's all-time major-league record with 802 pitching appearances for one club in a special fanfare on August 31, 1968. Steve Blass, the starting pitcher that night, retired the first hitter of the visiting Atlanta Braves. Manager Larry Shepard called "time out" and sent Blass out to left field in a prearranged scenario. In came ElRoy Face to pitch to one batter—Felix Millan. Face did his job well, getting Millan to ground out. Manager Shepard ordered Blass to return to the mound. ElRoy Face left for the Pirates' dugout to a standing ovation by the fans, who shouted their appreciation of the relief specialist who had given them so many thrills over the years. Blass concluded the game with an 8-0 whitewash of the Braves.

In an ironic twist of fate, earlier that same day ElRoy Face was sold to the Detroit Tigers.

# Tim Foli

Infielder Tim Foli made a tremendous impression on Pirate fans when he played for the Bucs from 1979-1981 and again in 1985. A deeply religious man, Foli added not only to the physical aspects of the game, but also to its character.

Although he wasn't gifted with long-ball power, Foli honed his ability to make contact with the ball and to make what are known as "productive outs"—grounding out in order to advance a runner, or hitting a sacrifice fly to score a run. His value became even more apparent when, in the 1979 World Series, he not only batted .333, but also went to the plate 33 times without striking out once. By doing so, he set a World Series record that stands to this day.

# Bob Friend

If there was ever an example of someone being in the wrong place at the wrong time, it was pitcher Bob Friend. The right-hander from Lafayette, Indiana, debuted with the Bucs in 1951, and he soon established himself as the team's ace. Had he pitched for a winning club, he would have racked up a lot more victories and gained increased national notoriety. Nonetheless, in 1955, this All-Star pitcher with a last-place team led the National League with a 2.84 ERA. That was the only time any pitcher won the ERA title with a cellar-dwelling club.

# Frankie Frisch

Hall of Famer Frankie Frisch managed the Pirates from 1940-1946. As an alumnus of the old "Gas House Gang" of the St. Louis Cardinals, Frisch learned never to back away from a confrontation, especially when it involved an umpire. He left no doubt in anyone's mind if he thought an arbiter made a poor decision. Once, when the umpires failed to call a game soon enough (in his opinion) during a heavy rainstorm, Frisch strolled out of the dugout wearing rubber boots and carrying an umbrella. That gesture earned him nothing more than an early exit from the game plus a healthy fine from the office of the Baseball Commissioner.

\* \* \*

Following another of his oft-repeated battles with umpires, this one peppered with expletives unacceptable even on a baseball diamond, manager Frisch was thumbed out of the game along with two of his players. The next day, the two players received a telegram from National League president Ford Frick telling them that they were fined $50 each.

"When I heard the news," said Frisch, "I was quite pleased that I had escaped. Two days later, I received a wire from Mr. Frick that read, 'Sorry I overlooked you. You're fined $75.'"

# Joe Garagiola

Before he became a national television personality, Joe Garagiola played nine years in the majors with four teams, including the Pittsburgh Pirates. During the disastrous 1952 campaign when his club lost 112 games during a 154-game season, Garagiola displayed his sparkling wit when he evaluated the talent on the team. "When we had a rainout, we held a victory dance."

He later said about the same group of players, "We were so bad, we deserved to end up ninth in an eight-team league."

\* \* \*

Garagiola thought he had heard every excuse in the book from a player who made an error. That is, until one night game during that infamous 1952 season when one of the infielders missed an easy ground ball that bounced right by him for a base hit.

When the team returned to the dugout following the final out of the inning, the veteran catcher approached the infielder who had just muffed the play.

"What happened out there?" he asked.

The response was one that still baffles him. The infielder

*Joe Garagiola kept his eyes on the ball and open
to funny things that happened on the playing field.*

looked Garagiola in the eye and said with the sincerity of one who actually believed what he was about to say, "I lost it in the moon."

* * *

The fact that the 1952 Pirates won only 42 games (the second fewest in club history, next to the 1890 team, which amassed only 23 victories), were dead last in the National League in batting average, earned run average and fielding percentage and ended the season in eighth place, 22 1/2 games behind seventh-place Boston, was not enough to keep Joe Garagiola from discovering something positive about the experience. "We had the most courageous team in baseball," he mused. "Think about it. We had 154 games scheduled and we showed up for every one of them."

Today, this oft-requested after-dinner speaker is not afraid to stretch the truth a wee bit when describing the '52 Bucs. "We had fans leave the ballpark before the game had ended, just like everyone else. But our fans even walked across the infield."

# Phil Garner

Phil Garner was a throwback to the old-time ballplayers who gave their all to win games. Because of his rugged approach to baseball and his willingness to play through injury, he was labeled "Scrap Iron" by the media and his teammates. As a player for the Bucs from 1977-1981, this spunky infielder helped the Bucs to a world championship in 1979 with a career-high .293 average.

His star shone brightest in the '79 World Series victory against the heavily favored Baltimore Orioles when he joined Pepper Martin (1931) and Johnny Lindell (1947) as the only players to bat .500 in a seven-game series.

# Brian Giles

When the Pirates got slugger Brian Giles in a trade with the Cleveland Indians before the 1999 season, the media and fans alike felt that this was one of the best swaps in Pirates history. When Giles hit .315 and smoked 39 homers that first year, their preliminary analysis was justified.

As a sign of their appreciation for his contributions to the club, Pirate management elected to host a "Brian Giles Bobblehead Doll Night" on September 6, 2002. More than 33,000 fans packed PNC Park to see the game against the Florida Marlins (won by the Bucs 11-0) and to take home one of the prized replicas of the productive left fielder.

A few weeks prior to the game, the aggressive Giles hit his head on the playing surface while trying to make a diving catch against the Dodgers in Los Angeles. "They'll have to put a lump on the forehead to make that doll authentic," he said.

Bobblehead dolls, a popular novelty throughout Major League Baseball, are, by their very nature, more symbolic than accurate in terms of likeness. According to Robert Dvorchak, veteran writer with the *Pittsburgh Post-Gazette*, when manager Lloyd McClendon was informed about the plan to create a Giles doll, he asked with a laugh, "Is it a short, stumpy little thing?" Later, word got around the clubhouse that it looked more like bullpen coach Bruce Tanner.

*For several seasons, slugger Brian Giles led the Bucs in nearly every offensive category.*

# Hank Greenberg

"Hammerin'" Hank Greenberg played his last big-league season with Pittsburgh in 1947. The American League home-run champion clubbed 44 homers and knocked in a league-leading 127 runs the previous year for the Detroit Tigers. His most productive year was in 1938, when he challenged the record of 60 homers from the bat of Babe Ruth by hitting 58 out of the park.

Greenberg was not eager to join the Pirates or any other team that season. He was hurt by the abrupt manner in which the Tigers had let him go, and seriously contemplated retiring from the game.

Pirates owner Frank McKinney and club treasurer John Galbreath put together a tempting package to lure Greenberg away from thoughts of a premature retirement. Included in their offer was an $80,000 salary (an astronomical amount in those days), a private hotel room while the team was on the road, a private car on trains while en route to other cities, and a race horse from the famous Darby Dan Farms owned by Mr. Galbreath.

The right-handed pull hitter was impressed with the deal, but still issued one more demand: the team had to shorten the distance between home plate and the left-field wall at Forbes Field. The Pirates agreed. To comply, they built a double bullpen

*Hank Greenberg was not only a powerful hitter, but also
a masterful teacher for younger hitters such as Ralph Kiner.*

that extended 200 feet from the left field bleachers in front of the huge scoreboard to a point in left center field. An eight-foot-high fence made of wood topped with wire mesh became the new left field wall.

The 30-foot area between the fence and the scoreboard was used as bullpens for relief pitchers for both sides. It was baptized "Greenberg Gardens" in honor of the new Pirates slugger.

Greenberg hit 25 homers that year. Outshining him and capturing most of the headlines that year, however, was one of Mr. Greenberg's star "pupils"—Ralph Kiner, who was the National League home run champion the year before with 23. Greenberg took the young Kiner under his wing and urged him to stand closer to the plate so that he could hit even an outside pitch with authority. Kiner listened carefully and applied the lessons from the sage veteran. That season, Kiner smacked 51 four-baggers to tie for the home run crown.

Hank Greenberg retired after that season. Meanwhile, Kiner continued to powder the ball out of the park. Appropriately, Greenberg Gardens soon became known as "Kiner's Korner."

Throughout the remaining years of his life as a baseball executive, Hank Greenberg remained grateful for the opportunity to play for the Pirates and to pass along his skills to Kiner. "However," he said, "I never did see that race horse."

# Dick Groat

Shortstop Dick Groat, a native of nearby Wilkensburg, has seen both good years and bad years with the Pittsburgh Pirates. While he may be best remembered as the captain of the world championship 1960 team, he was also part of the squad during the middle '50s when the only realistic goal was to stay out of last place.

None of these firsthand experiences would have been possible had Groat pursued another sport in which he excelled—basketball. At Duke University, he was selected as College Player of the Year in 1951 when he scored a school-record 831 points. After graduation, Groat was the first player to have his uniform number (10) retired by the school.

He captured the eye of scouts from the National Basketball Association and played professional basketball for the Fort Wayne Pistons, averaging nearly 12 points a game. He also was drafted by the Pirates.

Professional basketball at that time offered little in terms of potential salary, and general manager Branch Rickey presented an ultimatum—choose either basketball or baseball. Dick Groat opted for baseball—a decision that definitely pleased Pirate fans.

During Dick Groat's second year with the club in 1955, the Pirates brought on board twin brothers Johnny and Eddie

O'Brien. Johnny had been a star basketball player, a two-time All-American guard. Eddie was also a solid player and joined his brother on the team.

Broadcaster Bob Prince observed that the Bucs, that year, could match the skills of most professional basketball teams. "It's just too bad we could not transfer that prowess onto the baseball diamond where it counted," he said.

# Harvey Haddix

Mention the name Harvey Haddix, and baseball fans everywhere think of the game on May 26, 1959, when the Pirates played the Milwaukee Braves at County Stadium in what the *Pittsburgh Sun-Telegraph* described the next day as "the greatest game of all time."

The 5'9" southpaw, nicknamed "The Kitten," was named by Pirate manager Danny Murtaugh to start the game against the ace right-hander of the Braves' staff—pitcher Lew Burdette.

Both Burdette and Haddix pitched extremely well that night, only Haddix pitched a wee bit better. Burdette scattered a few hits and did not allow a Pirate to cross the plate after nine innings. Haddix, in the same span of innings, allowed no hits; in fact, he did not allow one Milwaukee batter to reach base. At the end of regulation play, he had equaled a major-league record by facing 27 batters without anyone getting aboard via a hit, a walk or an error. In the history of Major League Baseball, this had happened only 10 times before. The last time was Don Larsen's perfect game in the 1956 World Series.

There was only one problem. The baseball game was still tied 0-0. Haddix, responding to the cheers of the partisan 19,194 Braves fans in attendance, shut down the opponents in the 10th inning.

*Harvey Haddix and the Braves' Joe Adcock were
key figures in one of baseball's most memorable games.*

And in the 11th inning.

And in the 12th inning.

Although Lew Burdette allowed 12 Pirate hits, none of the Bucs scored.

Had Harvey Haddix been a superstitious man, he might have asked to be taken out before the bottom half of the 13th inning. But he felt up to the task.

The fans cheered so loudly as Haddix stepped onto the mound, an outsider would have thought that they were encouraging a hometown pitcher. The cheers suddenly ceased when a routine grounder by Felix Mantilla to third baseman Don Hoak resulted in an erroneous throw into the dirt that bounced off the glove of first baseman Glenn "Rocky" Nelson. When Umpire Frank Dascoli barked "Safe!" the Braves had a runner on base for the first time in two hours, 50 minutes.

The Milwaukee crowd now sensed a potential victory and directed their cheers toward their home team. A sacrifice bunt, followed by an intentional walk to Hank Aaron, put two men on base with one out. Slugger Joe Adcock then swung his 42-ounce bat at a 1-0 pitch and sent the ball over the 375-foot mark in right center field for what should have been a home run—the first hit of the game—giving the Braves an apparent 3-0 win.

Aaron, however, thought the ball had bounced into the stands for a ground-rule double. As a result, he rounded second base in a nonchalant fashion and headed for the dugout. Adcock, meanwhile, kept circling the bases and crossed home plate.

National League president Warren Giles reviewed films of the game the next day and ruled that Adcock was out, because he passed Aaron on the base paths. He awarded Adcock a double and declared that the final score was Milwaukee 1, Pittsburgh 0.

It was a bizarre ending to one of the classic baseball games of all time.

\* \* \*

Something that many people might not know about the famous game pitched by Harvey Haddix was that prior to his

May 26, 1959 masterpiece, the 155-pound native of Medway, Ohio, nearly volunteered to sit out the game due to a nagging flu that had sapped his body of strength for a full week. Prior to the contest, he promised manager Danny Murtaugh that he would give it his best for as long as his body would hold out.

\* \* \*

Was Harvey Haddix exceptionally nervous during his 12-inning perfect game?

"Somewhat," answered Haddix. "I knew it was a no-hitter—knew it all the time. I did not know I had a perfect game. I thought I might have walked a man somewhere along the line."

\* \* \*

The day following his unforgettable pitching performance, Haddix received a pointed telegram from his fraternity at college. All the message said was:

"Dear Harvey, Tough S—!"

"At first, I was really disturbed about the message," confessed Haddix. "Then I thought about it for a few minutes and decided: Yeah. That says it all."

\* \* \*

Placed into the category entitled: "This could never happen, but it did," right after his 12-inning perfect game, a newspaper reporter asked Harvey Haddix: "Would you say, Harvey, that this was the best game you ever pitched?"

# Fred Haney

Taking the reins as Pirates manager in 1953 was the genial Fred Haney. It was not a position for which applicants stood in line. Haney inherited a team that had lost 112 the year before and was given little, if any, new blood. His '53 Pirates continued the slump of the year before, losing 104 games. It was a team that, from the first inning of Opening Day, posed no genuine threat to the rest of the National League.

The fans knew this. The media knew this. The players themselves knew this.

As the season wore on, some of the disgruntled players attempted to "escape" the realities of the baseball world through excessive use of alcohol.

One relief pitcher, whose name will remain in confidence, was one of the few non-drinkers on the team. The mounting frustrations eventually got the best of him and he decided to join his brethren in washing away his troubles by partaking in some serious drinking on the night before a scheduled game the next afternoon in St. Louis.

St. Louis is a wonderful city, but in August it can be a most miserable experience, especially if the temperature and humidity are high and the air becomes stagnant.

*General manager Branch Rickey (left) looked for some
miracles along with manager Fred Haney and traveling
secretary Bob Rice during spring training prior to the 1953 season.*

The combination of heat, moisture and excess booze eventually took their toll on the pitcher—a rookie to the perils of alcohol—the next morning. His head ached, and his tongue tasted like the bottom of a birdcage. He could not eat breakfast; he just lay in bed watching the ceiling of his hotel room spin. When he reached the ballpark and changed into his uniform, he could barely walk a straight line out to the bullpen.

By the seventh inning, the Pirates trailed by a score of 9-1. Fred Haney called on the obviously affected pitcher to warm up. Five minutes later, Haney signaled the bullpen and summoned the still-bewildered pitcher.

The pitcher, now perspiring and weak from his bout the previous evening with John Barleycorn, walked the first batter he faced, then gave up singles to the next two. With the game now far out of reach, Manager Haney called time and walked slowly to the mound. Frankly, the pitcher was grateful; he looked forward to a refreshing shower. The sage Haney, keenly aware of what had happened the night before, merely put his hand on the shoulder of the rookie and said, "I just came out to tell you that I am *not* taking you out. In fact, I'm ordering you to finish the game."

When his manager turned and retreated to the dugout, the pitcher felt sicker than he had ever been. From that day forward, none of his teammates ever saw him even sip another drop of alcohol.

# Don Hoak

Scrappy Don Hoak, a steady third baseman for the Bucs from 1959-1962, was instrumental in helping the Bucs win the National League pennant and World Series in 1960. He had a reputation for losing his cool during games and was a thorn in the flesh of many umpires. At the same time, he was a quick thinker when the situation demanded. Once, that thinking resulted in the addition of a new rule for Major League Baseball.

Just before he joined the Pirates organization, when he was playing for Cincinnati, Hoak and another Red were on base with no outs. The next batter hit a ground ball to short that should have been an easy double play. Hoak realized that if he, as a runner, got hit with the ball, he would be out, but at least he could prevent a double play.

Hoak not only allowed the ball to hit him, he actually fielded it with his bare hands, then nonchalantly tossed it Milwaukee Braves shortstop Johnny Logan.

That last gesture drew the ire of the baseball commissioner, but Hoak wasn't fined; technically he had broken no official rule. Both the American and National Leagues subsequently ruled that in the case of willful interference, both the batter and runner are out.

# Ralph Kiner

During the "Kiner Era" of the Pirates (1946-1953), the team was a viable contender for the pennant in only one season (1948). The other times, they were cellar-dwellers or close to it. The only drawing card at this time was the young left fielder who set a record for leading the National League in home runs seven years in a row.

Fans came to the ballpark two hours early just to see him take batting practice. During the game, even if the score was lopsided in favor of the opposing team, people waited until Kiner's last at-bat before leaving. Conversations around the water coolers at work the next morning did not begin with: "How did the Pirates do last night?" Instead, most people asked: "How did Kiner do?"

\* \* \*

Some astute observers rank the 1952 Pirates as among the worst teams in the history of Major League Baseball. With a last-place record of 42-112, the team posed little threat to the opposition. The only bright spot in the season was the fact that slugger Ralph Kiner led the league in homers for the seventh straight season with 37.

*Ralph Kiner is greeted by teammates following
one of the 301 home runs he slammed as a Pirate.*

When he met with Branch Rickey—the team's vice president and general manager—to sign a contract for the next season, Kiner was shocked to see an offer that included a 25-percent cut from his previous salary of $90,000.

"Why do I get a cut?" asked the mild-mannered slugger. "I led the league last year in home runs."

Rickey raised one of his bushy eyebrows, took a trademark cigar out of his mouth and pointed it in Kiner's direction. "Let me ask you, son. Where did we finish last year?"

"Ahhh, in last place, Mr. Rickey," Kiner answered.

"Hummmmmmm," responded Rickey. "Well, let me tell you something. Son, we could have finished last without you."

When Mr. Rickey replaced the cigar in his mouth, Kiner knew the conversation had ended. He signed the contract—his last with the Pirates.

\* \* \*

Ralph Kiner has been rumored to have once said, "Singles hitters drive Fords; home run hitters drive Cadillacs." The truth of the matter is that he never said it. Instead, it was an observation given to a reporter by a teammate—pitcher Fritz Ostermueller.

\* \* \*

During the final months of the 1949 season, Ralph Kiner clubbed one of his 54 homers that year into Wrigley Field's left-field bleachers. Cubs manager Frankie Frisch went to the mound and gave his pitcher, Bob Muncrief, some sage advice: "Never give Kiner a curve. Throw him nothing but fastballs." On Kiner's next plate appearance, Muncrief heeded his manager's advice and threw a fastball high and inside. Kiner swung and sent a skyrocket over the bleachers onto Waveland Avenue. When Frisch went to the mound to call for a relief pitcher, Muncrief tried to make the best of the situation. "Well, Skip," said the exiting pitcher, "he hit yours a lot farther than he hit mine."

\* \* \*

The 1951 season was just two months old when Ralph Kiner and fellow outfielder Wally Westlake were asked by Branch Rickey to accompany him to a luncheon for the famous Duquesne Club at a Pittsburgh hotel, at which Rickey was scheduled to speak. Both agreed.

During his presentation, Mr. Rickey solicited questions from the audience. One man asked about whether or not he would consider making some blockbuster trades that year. Mr. Rickey responded, "I am always looking for ways to improve my team. But I can assure you that as long as I am with the Pittsburgh Pirates, I shall never trade the two men who are sitting alongside of me. We will continue to build the team around Misters Kiner and Westlake."

"The next week," Kiner recalls, "Wally Westlake was shipped off to St. Louis. I knew then that my time with Pittsburgh was limited."

He was right. Two years later, Kiner was traded to Chicago.

\* \* \*

The day following the trade of Ralph Kiner to the Chicago Cubs, the Pirates realized that since their greatest home run threat no longer wore the black and gold of the Bucs, the opposition might get much more use out of the shortened left field fence dubbed "Kiner's Korner." They immediately announced plans to dismantle the structure made of wood and wire and expand the left field wall by 30 feet.

When he caught wind of this proposed change, baseball commissioner Ford C. Frick called a halt to the idea and ordered the structure to remain intact until the end of the season.

\* \* \*

In spite of his status as a superstar in the late '40s and early '50s, Ralph Kiner never refused to give a youngster an autograph at the ballpark. He asked only that the boys and girls line up in an orderly fashion and behave themselves.

Why was Kiner so considerate? The reason stemmed from an incident that happened when he was a young lad in his early teens. While living in Alhambra, California, he happened to see Dizzy Dean, the famous pitcher of the St. Louis Cardinals, at spring training. Ralph was carrying with him a baseball—not uncommon for him at the time. He approached the legendary pitcher and asked for an autograph. Dean, however, brushed him aside and refused to sign anything.

While he was standing there, still holding the unsigned ball, young Ralph felt miserable because of the treatment he had just received. "At that moment," says Kiner, "I vowed that if ever I became a major-league ballplayer, I would never, ever, make a kid feel as bad as I felt right then."

# Bruce Kison

Relief specialist Bruce Kison enjoyed a fine rookie season with the Bucs in 1971. He compiled a winning record (6-5) and a 3.41 ERA. As frosting on the cake, he was part of a world championship team (the Bucs defeated heavily favored Baltimore four games to three, and Kison pitched 6.1 innings of one-hit ball, winning Game 4), and he got married.

Pitching was, indeed, a strong suit for Kison. Making schedules was not. For some unexplained reason, the 21-year-old right-hander arranged for his wedding to take place on the same day as Game 7 of the World Series. On top of this, the game was held in Baltimore; his wedding was planned for Pittsburgh.

Immediately after the Pirates won the final contest by a score of 4-1, Kison did not have the luxury of popping champagne corks with his teammates. Instead, he and his best man, pitcher Bob Moose, rushed to a waiting helicopter sitting in the parking lot of Memorial Stadium and were whisked away to a private jet waiting for them at the airport. The bridegroom and best man arrived at the church only 20 minutes late.

It wasn't until years later that the media learned that the transportation and details were arranged by Pirates broadcaster Bob Prince.

# Mike LaValliere

Mike "Spanky" LaValliere, a catcher for the Pirates from 1987-1992, may best be remembered for one of the last times he touched a baseball for the Bucs.

LaValliere was not only a superb catcher, but a fan favorite as well. Part of the reason was that he was one person with whom fans could identify. When he walked onto the baseball diamond, the portly, 5'8" backstop was not a poster child for a professional athlete; he looked, instead, more like your favorite uncle.

On October 14, 1992, the Pirates and the Atlanta Braves deadlocked going into the deciding game in a best-of-seven National League Championship Series at Atlanta's Fulton County Stadium. Manager Bobby Cox's Braves had some fine players on its roster, including David Justice, Greg Maddux, Tom Glavine and former Pirate Sid Bream, who had a serious leg injury that hampered his ability to run. The Pirates also fielded a superb team—Barry Bonds, Andy Van Slyke, Don Slaught, Lloyd McClendon, Doug Drabek and Bob Walk—who gave their fans hope that this would be the year for their first World Series appearance in 13 years.

Down three games to one, the Pirates rallied, as they did so many times that year, to knot the series at three games apiece.

Going into the bottom of the ninth in Game 7, the Pirates were coasting with a 2-0 lead behind the superb pitching of their ace, Doug Drabek. But the Braves' bats came alive. A leadoff double, an infield error and a walk to Sid Bream loaded the bases with no outs. Atlanta fans intoned their famous "tomahawk chant." Pirate manager Jim Leyland called in relief pitcher Stan Belinda to squelch the Braves' rally.

Leyland's strategy seemed to work when Belinda got the next batter on a sacrifice fly. With the score 2-1, he walked the next hitter on four pitches. Braves fans chanted with even more gusto, but a pop fly to short for out number two quieted their enthusiasm. Only one out and one batter—pinch hitter Francisco Cabrera (who had only three hits all year long)—separated the Bucs from a trip to the World Series.

On a 2-1 count, Cabrera defied the odds and lined a single to left. The runner on third base scored the tying run, and Sid Bream hobbled on his bad leg around third. Left fielder Barry Bonds fielded the ball and, like everyone else in the stadium, seemed surprised to see the injured Bream attempting to score. He uncorked a throw to LaValliere, who waited at the plate as a limping Bream and the ball raced toward the plate. LaValliere caught the ball. Bream slid. LaValliere reached out as far as he could. He was a fraction of a second too late. Umpire Randy Marsh's call: "Safe!"

The Braves won the game 3-2 and went on to face Toronto in the 1992 World Series.

Commenting on that close call at the plate, LaValliere said, "I don't know if he was out or if he was safe. The throw was up the line a bit. I'm five feet eight, but this time I was a half-inch too short. If I'm five feet eight and a half, he's out. Bream's out."

Following that game, a sad Mike LaValliere returned to the Pirates' locker room, showered, and changed into his street clothes. He played in only one game the next year for the Pirates before going to the Chicago White Sox.

# Vernon Law

One of the most sought-after recruits in the late '40s was a teenage pitcher from Meridian, Idaho, named Vernon Law. The Pirates got him with the help of some calculated cunning.

Scouts from a variety of teams were in Meridian one day to visit the parents of the fireballing right-hander. Included among the team representatives were Babe Herman and Herman Welker of the Pirates. On the pretense of offering assistance to the other scouts, Welker advised them the night before their visits that one sure way to gain favor with Vernon's father was to take him a box of cigars. After thanking the Pirate scout for his kindness, the other representatives marched with confidence to the Law household at a preappointed time the next morning and proudly held out the cigars as a token of their appreciation.

Mr. and Mrs. Law, however, were not impressed. As faithful members of the Church of Jesus Christ of Latter Day Saints (the Mormons), both abhorred smoking. These scouts didn't stand a chance.

Later that same morning, in stark contrast, Welker and Herman brought a box of candy for Mrs. Law. She warmly welcomed them into her home. While they were chatting, the telephone rang. A strange, but familiar voice asked for Mrs. Law. It was Bing Crosby—a minority owner of the Pirates. He spoke with

*Pirates captain Dick Groat (right) shows pitcher Vernon Law—starter for the first game of the '60 World Series—that he and his bat will support Law. It must have worked. Law and the Bucs won that first game, 6-4.*

her for about 15 minutes. He told her what a fine addition her son would be to the Pirates and promised that the organization would do everything in its power to ensure a wholesome atmosphere for young Vernon. "She almost fainted on the spot from excitement," recalls Vernon.

"I almost felt guilty pulling that trick on the scouts from the other teams," confessed Welker. "*Almost* felt guilty," he emphasized with a broad grin.

\* \* \*

Vernon Law, Cy Young Award winner in 1960 for his splendid 20-9 season with a league-leading 18 complete games, was a devout Mormon who personified a virtuous life. At the same time, if an opposing batter stood too close to the plate, Law had no qualms about brushing him back with a high inside fastball.

During one game, the limits of his aggressiveness were put to the test. After one of the Pirate's batters was struck by a pitched ball, manager Danny Murtaugh ordered Vernon to knock down the first batter for the other team "just to send a message."

Vernon felt he could not do that. "Skip," he said, "it's against my religion. The Bible, after all, says, 'Turn the other cheek.'"

Murtaugh replied, "It'll cost you $500 if you don't knock him down."

Law paused for a second, then said, "The Bible also says, 'He who lives by the sword shall also die by the sword.'"

\* \* \*

Those of us who have seen baseball played only over the past 20 years or so have become used to the fact that most starting pitchers are expected to last six, perhaps seven innings. Prior to this time, starting pitchers took pride in being able to complete all nine innings.

One modern-day Pirate did that not just once, but twice, in one evening.

On July 19, 1955, Vernon Law took the mound against the Milwaukee Braves at Forbes Field following only three days' rest. Originally scheduled to pitch that evening was Ron "The Callery, PA, Hummer" Kline. A sore shoulder sidelined Kline that evening, so manager Fred Haney asked if Law could fill in. Law agreed, and Manager Haney promised to relieve him if he got tired.

Law worked all nine innings, allowing just two runs. Unfortunately, that's all the Pirates got as well. Law went out and shut out the Braves in the 10th.

And the 11th.

And the 12th.

And the 13th.

And the 14th . . . the 15th . . . the 16th . . . the 17th . . . the 18th.

An appreciative crowd cheered Law as he left the mound following the last out in the top of the 18th. They knew they had seen something spectacular. Vernon Law had pitched the equivalent of two complete games in one evening. Nobody had ever come close to equaling that performance in big-league history.

In the top of the 19th, reliever Bob Friend gave up a run. But the Bucs responded with two in the home half of the inning to eke out a 4-3 win.

In the next morning's edition of the *Pittsburgh Post-Gazette*, veteran sportswriter Al Abrams wrote, "He wasn't around when the 4-3 victory was pulled out of the smoldering embers of defeat in the 19th inning, but Vernon Law turned in a performance the equal of which the great pitching titans of the past would have been proud to call their own."

# Tommy Leach

"Wee" (5' 6 1/2", 150 pounds) Tommy Leach spent most of his 19 big-league years with the Pirates as an infielder. In 1902 he led the National League with only six home runs—the lowest number of home runs ever to lead the league in modern-day baseball. The amazing fact was that none of his home runs ever left the ballpark.

The Pirates played their home games that year in Exposition Park—a mammoth field even by today's standards. The right field and left field lines were 400 feet; it was 450 feet to dead center, providing a definite challenge to any hitter in the so-called "Dead Ball Era." For the speedy Leach, however, this became a genuine plus. If he was fortunate enough to hit a ball between outfielders, chances are the ball would continue rolling far enough and long enough to allow him to circle the bases for an inside-the-park home run.

# Jim Leyland

Perhaps the most demanding and frustrating position on a Major League Baseball team is field manager. It is here that you are compelled to work with 25 gifted athletes, most of whom show up on the first day of spring training embodying equally strong egos.

None ever knew this better than Jim Leyland—manager of the Pirates from 1986 to 1996. His greatest challenge was, as might be expected, the outspoken left-fielder Barry Bonds who seldom left any doubt as to how he felt about any subject, including his fellow teammates.

Loaded with talent, Bonds was a two-time All Star and twice voted the league's Most Valuable Player. Unfortunately, he had a gruff personality that seemed to turn off a lot of fans and teammates. In short, he would never win a "Mr. Congeniality Award."

Manager Jim Leyland took a much more positive approach with Bonds. In an interview with veteran sportscaster Bob Costas, he said: "I saw a lot of good things in Barry. He's not as tough as he lets on. I think he's one of those guys for whom it was a motivational tool to upset people.

"He was coachable and he was manageable. A lot of people didn't think so, but it depended on how you coached him. Barry was one of those guys where he was very coachable, but you had to let him think it was his idea."

Hmmmm. It makes you wonder if Jim Leyland was able to get so much from someone with the temperament of Barry Bonds, has he ever considered taking a job in national politics?

# Dale Long

"Curtain calls" are rather common in today's baseball games. If a player hits a dramatic home run or performs another kind of spectacular feat, fans cheer until he comes out of the dugout to "take a bow."

That tradition, however, is relatively new when compared with others in America's pastime. It began in Pittsburgh on Monday, May 28, 1956, before a capacity crowd at Forbes Field in a game against the Brooklyn Dodgers.

Dale Long, a consistent long-ball-hitting first baseman for the Bucs, two days earlier had tied a major-league record by hitting a home run in his seventh consecutive game. Forbes Field that night overflowed with zealous fans who came for one reason—to see Long break that record. The evening before, the frenzy received even more national attention when Long was a featured guest on *The Ed Sullivan Show* on CBS—an appearance made possible due to the rainout of a doubleheader in Philadelphia that afternoon. That set the stage for Long's attempt to break the record before a hometown audience.

Pitching for the Dodgers that evening was Carl Erskine—a future Hall of Fame right-hander—who had tossed a no-hitter against the Giants just 16 days earlier.

*Dale Long is greeted warmly by his teammates following his record-setting home run in eight straight games.*

On his first trip to the plate that night, Long tapped an Erskine curveball into the dirt for a weak groundout. Pirate fans groaned. On his second time at bat, Long gave the fans the one thing they came to see. He swung hard at another curveball and hit it over the 27-foot-high mesh screen deep into the right field stands. As Long circled the bases following his record-breaking smash, fans screamed with delight.

The next Pirates batter, Bob Skinner, knowing he would be unable to concentrate during the clamor, refused to step into the batter's box. Instead, he stood, leaning on his bat, and stared into the dugout. The fans continued to cheer with increased vigor. Nobody moved. The game was held up for a full ten minutes until one of his teammates pushed Long out of the dugout for his well-deserved bow.

Two other players—Ken Griffey, Jr., and Don Mattingly have since equaled Long's record.

The Pirates won the game that night by a score of 3-2, but the most memorable events of the game will be Dale Long's record-setting home run and the first encore ever called for in the history of Major League Baseball.

# Connie Mack

Not many people know that Hall of Famer Connie Mack's real name was Cornelius Alexander McGillicuddy. Not many people know, also, that he was a catcher with the Pittsburgh Ball Club from 1891-1896 and was player/manager for his last two-plus years.

In his first full season as manager, Mack did whatever it took to win ball games. One story that he never denied was that on the night prior to a home game, he placed some baseballs in a freezer in order to "freeze the life out of the balls." This was during the time when foul balls were tossed back onto the field to be reused. When the opposing team was at bat and a ball was hit onto the roof of the stadium, a young boy stationed there to retrieve foul balls would toss back toward the field of play one of the chilled balls he had gotten from Mr. Mack in lieu of the one actually hit on the roof. The "frozen ball" made it more difficult for any batter to get substantial distance on the ball in the event he got a solid hit on the next pitch.

# Rabbit Maranville

Hall of Famer Walter James Vincent "Rabbit" Maranville played four of his big-league years with Pittsburgh from 1921-1924. Although the 5'5", 155-pound infielder never hit .300 in a season, he was a feisty player who was one of the first to demonstrate the importance of solid defense in building a winning team. He was also a jokester both on and off the field—something that gave his managers, and sometimes umpires, fits.

One day when the Bucs were playing in Philadelphia, Maranville was on first as a result of a walk on four borderline pitches. Phillies manager Art Fletcher screamed in protest to home plate umpire Charles "Cy" Pfirman. Fletcher's words got stronger. Pfirman countered with stronger, more pointed expletives. Finally, Pfirman had had enough and tossed the Phillies' manager out of the game.

Instead of leaving quietly, Manager Fletcher clenched his fists, darted from the dugout toward home plate and threw a "haymaker" at Pfirman. Pfirman swung back in self-defense. Bob Hart, the first base umpire, quickly ran to Pfirman's aid and ended up between his colleague and Fletcher. Following a lot of swinging and pushing, the fight came to a quick end when Pfirman smacked Fletcher over the head with his heavy mask.

Once order was restored, the umpires returned to their positions.

Maranville, still standing on first base, turned to Hart and said, "Bob, your face is all bloodied up. Wait a minute and I'll get some Mercurochrome for you." But Bob Hart did not have as much as a scratch on him. Maranville yelled to the bench, "Hey, bring out that Mercurochrome." He then painted Hart's face until the unsuspecting umpire looked like a zebra.

"The next day when Bob Hart came on to the field," said Maranville, "he came over to me, and what he called me I dare not repeat in mixed company."

# Bill Mazeroski

William Stanley Mazeroski, whose hard-nosed hustle earned him eight Gold Glove Awards during his 17-year career with the Bucs (1956-1972), helped lead the Pirates to three division titles, two National League pennants and two World Series championships. He's best remembered in Pirates history for his dramatic, ninth-inning home run on October 13, 1960, that gave the Bucs their first World Series trophy since 1925.

Mazeroski's brilliance, however, was not in the batter's box. Instead, it was at second base, where he set the standard for fielding the keystone sack, especially in turning double plays.

The so-called "experts" in baseball are more easily impressed with batting averages and home runs than they are with fielding. Consequently, Maz was not voted into the Hall of Fame during his first year of eligibility. Pittsburgh fans and the local media, however, refused to lose hope. Through a vigorous campaign for his induction, they finally got their wish in 2001.

While there's no doubt that Maz was one of the most brilliant infielders ever to play Major League Baseball, his skills as a world-class orator were tested during his induction speech into the Hall on August 5, 2001. The honest simplicity of this coal miner's son shone through as he delivered his tear-filled address. Part of what he said was:

"I've got twelve pages here. That's not like me. I'll probably skip half of it and get halfway through this thing and quit. Anyhow. . . I think defense belongs in the Hall of Fame. Defense deserves as much credit as pitching and hitting. . . This is going to be hard, so I probably won't say about half of this stuff. I thought when the Pirates retired my number that that would be the greatest thing to ever happen to me. It's hard to top this. I don't think I'm gonna make it. I think you can kiss these twelve pages down the drain. I want to thank everybody. . . I want to thank all the friends and family that have made this long trip here to listen to me speak and hear this crap. Thank you very, very much. Thanks everybody. That's enough."

\* \* \*

What did Maz do following his dramatic game-winning home run in the 1960 World Series? While many of his champagne-soaked teammates joined in the hoopla in the streets of Pittsburgh, he and his wife, Milene, retreated to Schenley Park to get away from it all. "Nobody was there," he recalls. "No cars. Even the squirrels had disappeared. Maybe they were all out celebrating."

\* \* \*

Before Forbes Field was torn down in 1971, the University of Pittsburgh purchased the property on which the ballpark stood. As a reminder of the memories generated from those once-hallowed grounds, three things remain for all loyal Pirate fans to see:

1.   A remnant of the center field wall that still contains the painted number 457 FT, showing the distance from home plate, complete with the flagpole that stood inside the wall;

2.   A metal plaque on the sidewalk marking the spot over which Maz hit his Series-winning homer in 1960;

3.   A glass-encased home plate in the floor of the lobby at the University of Pittsburgh's Posvar Hall, where a posted sign

*"Maz" kisses the home run bat that now rests in baseball's Hall of Fame.*

explains that this is the spot where major-league batters stood from 1909-1970.

While the remembrances are appreciated, the sign identifying home plate is not entirely accurate. Architects of the building confirm that the location of the plate was moved. Had they placed home plate in the exact spot it appeared on the field, it would have to be displayed in the fifth stall of the ladies' restroom.

\* \* \*

Since 1985, loyal Pirates fans have gathered at the remaining center field wall in Pittsburgh's Oakland section each October 13 to relive what many regard as the most glorious moment in Pirates history. Nobody is there to sell tickets. That would be akin to selling tickets to church. The only money spent may be for a hot dog from a nearby vendor. A jokester in the group asks if anyone who bet on the Yankees would like to double his bet. The people laugh; the excitement continues to build.

At precisely 1:05 p.m.—the time Game 7 began—someone begins to play a tape recording of the radio broadcast of that splendid contest. Longtime Pirates fans relish each unforgettable moment as if it were a religious experience—the freak ground ball that knocked Yankee shortstop Tony Kubek out of the game . . . the Hal Smith homer . . . the instinctive dive back into first by Mickey Mantle. And, of course, at 3:36 in the afternoon, when Maz slams the dramatic home run, the fans scream, leap for joy, exchange hugs and give themselves one more opportunity to celebrate the most important baseball moment in their lives.

Concluding the informal festivities, a member of the faithful flock yells out a quote familiar to all Pirate fans who listened to announcer Bob Prince: "We had 'em all the way!"

\* \* \*

One of the nicknames given Bill Mazeroski by his teammates and those who, on a regular basis, watched him play was "No Touch" because of his uncanny ability to catch and release a ball in one apparent motion. "It was as if his hands never touched the ball," said Pirates captain Dick Groat.

This talent was of tremendous benefit when Mazeroski had to take a ball from shortstop and relay it to first for a double play. Veteran baseball writer Bob Carroll, author of *When the Grass was Real,* echoed this appreciation when he referred to Maz as "The DaVinci of the double play."

\* \* \*

Most astute observers of the game of baseball agree with fellow Hall of Famer Brooks Robinson, who says that Bill Mazeroski set the standard for playing second base. Someone suggested that Maz exited the womb wearing an infielder's mitt. His training habits, however, left something to be desired. Manny Sanguillen recalls, "When some of us would meet about 8:00 in the morning and go out to eat breakfast, everybody ordered eggs or milk or oatmeal. Mazeroski would ask for two Iron Citys and a large Kielbasa sausage."

\* \* \*

"As an eight-year-old Yankee fan in 1960, I literally wept when Bill Mazeroski's home run cleared the ivy-covered wall of Forbes Field. Now, I believe I've come to terms with it and can see Bill Mazeroski for what he really was—one of baseball's all-time great second basemen."
—Bob Costas, NBC Sports

\* \* \*

Whatever happened to the baseball that Maz hit to end the 1960 World Series? Based on the fact that people have received over one million dollars for home run balls of lesser significance, it may be surprising to learn that when the teenager who retrieved the ball brought it back to the locker room to give to Pittsburgh's newest hero, Maz thanked him, signed the prized souvenir and gave it back to the young man. "Here, you keep it," he said. "The memory is good enough for me."

# Kevin McClatchy

In 1996, 32-year-old Kevin McClatchy, a member of the famed Sacramento, California newspaper family, purchased the Pittsburgh Baseball Club for a reported $90 million. Close friends advised him that he was tossing his money down the drain. Their observation seemed logical at the time. Baseball had still not completely recovered from the funk caused by a strike two years earlier. Also, since Pittsburgh was a comparatively small market, rumors circulated around town that the Pirates would be forced to move to a larger city just to be competitive economically.

McClatchy, however, galvanized his gumption and revealed his vision for a new ballpark and a more competitive team. To emphasize his intent, he penned something he called *The Bucs Fans Bill of Rights* that read:

1.  We pledge to follow a proven model to rebuild this franchise into a championship team.

2.  We pledge to keep baseball affordable for everyone in Pittsburgh, especially families.

3.  We pledge to work to secure a private-public financing package to build a new baseball-only ballpark in Pittsburgh.

4.  We pledge to make baseball fun in Pittsburgh.

5.  We pledge to work with area youth organizations to encourage baseball enthusiasm.

6.   We pledge to work with local officials to explore new transportation plans so that everyone can come to see the Pirates.

7.   We pledge to work with the Pittsburgh business community to make Pirates baseball a greater economic plus for the region.

8.   We pledge to talk Pirates baseball as often as we can to anyone who will listen.

9.   We pledge that we will do anything we can to cultivate your trust and support of the Pirates.

10. We pledge that we will not move the Pirates from Pittsburgh.

*Kevin McClatchy kept the Pirates in Pittsburgh.*

# Kevin McClatchy
## (part 2)

In September 2012, former controlling owner of the Pirates (1996-2007), Kevin McClatchy, made an announcement that he feared would heap criticism upon him and his beloved Pirates. In an interview published in *The New York Times*, the popular McClatchy, who was credited with being the most influential member of the Buc's front office in retaining the ball club for the Steel City, revealed his sexuality.

Kevin McCarthy boldly proclaimed publicly for the first time that he was gay.

He noted that suspicions emerged during his tenure with the Pirates in the executive office. "I would think quite a few [were suspicious]. Nobody would ask. Media never asked. ... Players didn't ask. I would get some mail that would insinuate that people heard rumors." In addition, he was the chairman of the board for the publishing giant— The McClatchy Co.— that owned several of the nation's more respected newspapers; as a result he was extremely wealthy. Pittsburghers, therefore, often asked why some young lady had not latched onto this young man who would have been a marvelous "catch" for even the most discriminating damsel.

That question was answered bluntly by the *Times* article.

McClatchy says he remained quiet about being gay for the years he owned the Pirates because "I was frightened that my own personal situation could in some way jeopardize the whole franchise. This, alone, convinced him that staying "closeted" was the best course of action at that time, he said. "Now," he says, "there's no way I want to go into the rest of my existence and ever have to hide my personal life again."

McClatchy, who sold his last shares of the Pirates in 2009, expected some backlash from those who wish he had spoken up sooner while he was in the thick of the trials and tribulations of a baseball owner. To the credit of the Pirate faithful, however, that seldom happened. Instead, today the vast majority of them still have only praise for Kevin McClatchy and for all he did to ensure that Major League Baseball would remain in Pittsburgh.

# Lloyd McClendon

Pirates manager Lloyd McClendon has been known to play aggressive, even creative baseball. However, he will probably never be so bold as to use the so-called "Zim theory of managing."

McClendon refers to the time he was playing for the Chicago Cubs in 1989, when they were managed by Don Zimmer. McClendon was at the plate with the bases loaded and only one out. Normal strategy called for McClendon to try and hit the ball somewhere into the outfield for either a hit or a sacrifice fly. McClendon and the runners, however, got the sign from Zimmer for a hit-and-run—where all the runners take off with pitch, hoping that the batter would hit the ball. However, were McClendon to swing and miss at the pitch, the runner coming in from third would be an easy out. In short, the strategy flew in the face of every bit of baseball common sense.

McClendon fouled off four straight pitches; each time the runners retreated to their bags, still shaking their heads in disbelief at the hit-and-run sign. On the next pitch, McClendon swung and laced a single to left field, scoring two runners.

After the side was retired and McClendon headed back to the dugout, Manager Zimmer told him, "I knew all along you were going to get a hit."

*Catcher (later Pirate manager) Lloyd McClendon was a
consistent hitter as well as a steady fixture behind the plate.*

McClendon responded, "But Skip, I sure didn't."

In spite of the success of the call, any time the bases are loaded for Pittsburgh, Lloyd McClendon swears he will never use what he calls the "Zim theory of managing."

# Andrew McCutchen

If you were to search the dictionary for a definition of the word "Humility," it wouldn't be surprising to find it accompanied by a photo of Pittsburgh Pirates center fielder Andrew McCutchen.

This talented athlete made a strong bid to win both the batting crown and the league's MVP in 2012 and was introduced in that same year to the media as a Gold-glove winner and earned the Silver Slugger Award. As a result of his heroic achievements, both as a consistent long-ball hitter at the plate and by thrilling fans with his circus catches in the field, he was rewarded by the club with a six-year $51.5 million contract.

Were you to ask Pirates fans and his teammates if he was worth this eye-popping salary, their collective answer would be a resounding "Yes."

Perhaps one of the compelling reasons for his popularity among both fans and colleagues lies not only in his skills on the baseball diamond, but in the attitude he displays everyday he's called upon to perform. Unlike far too many other players who might be classified as "super stars," McCutchen reflects a positive outlook on every dimension of life. He is unashamed to admit that he is truly fortunate to be a professional baseball player in the National League.

Much of the reason for this uncharacteristic (and refreshing) approach to the game and to his surroundings came from the beginning of his personal rags-to-riches adventure.

Illustrating this fact was a recent tweet sent over the Internet of a photo of McCutchen standing in front of his boyhood home—located in a trailer park in Bartow, Florida.

In an interview with *Sporting News* he spoke of living in the tiny trailer. He shared it with his parents and baby sister, with whom he shared a tiny bedroom while his father worked long hours in the nearby phosphate mines and struggled to eke out an existence for his family. It was here, he says, that he learned the value of hard work and of never taking anything for granted. "You're never too big or too busy to step back and give thanks for what you have. I always want to remember where I came from and the good things in life," he says. "And I'm not going to forget what got me here."

Andrew McCutchen ended his tweet with this reflection that shows the sort of humility that cannot be faked. "I've come a long way since living here," he wrote. "Thank God for all He's done in my life. Amen."

# George Metkovich

Symbolic of the sort of play and luck shared by the Pirates of the grim clubs in the early 1950s was a journeyman outfielder, George "Catfish" Metkovich. This California native, who once confessed to the Pittsburgh media that he would much rather have been a Hollywood actor than a major-league ballplayer, played in more than 1,000 games over a 10-year career. He therefore should have had some hands-on experience with the finer points of the game. If so, on one evening, all of his experience seemed to disappear, particularly when it involved baserunning fundamentals.

In one game during their fabled 1952 season, the Pirates were locked in a 3-3 tie with the Brooklyn Dodgers in the bottom of the ninth at Forbes Field. After two quick outs, Bobby Del Greco hit a single to center, and Metkovich surprised everyone in the stadium when he sent a ground ball to right past the outstretched glove of Jackie Robinson, moving Del Greco to third. With the fans cheering in anticipation of seeing one of the few Pirate wins that year, Gus Bell lined a shot to center field that sent Del Greco home with what appeared to be the winning run.

Metkovich joined in the celebration by leaping for joy between first and second base and returning to the Pirate dugout to join his teammates, who were exchanging handshakes and pats on the backs.

Seeing what was happening, Dodger manager Charlie Dressen shouted to center fielder Duke Snider to toss the ball to second base. There, shortstop Pee Wee Reese awaited the throw, then calmly stepped on second to complete the force play on Metkovich, who was now headed for the locker room.

The umpires called the Pirates back onto the field and informed them that Metkovich was out and, as a result, Del Greco's run did not count.

The Dodgers added two more runs in the top half of the tenth, which were enough to win the game 5-3. Thus, the '52 Pirates discovered a new way to lose a ballgame.

* * *

During one particularly forgettable afternoon during the '52 season at Chicago's Wrigley Field, Metkovich and the Pirates were being pummeled by the Cubs. First baseman Metkovich felt the brunt of the Chicago attack as he vainly tried to snare one line drive after another that whizzed by his outstretched glove. After about the third sharp hit had sailed into the outfield grass, a frustrated Metkovich shouted to first base umpire Lon Warneke, "For cryin' out loud, don't just stand there. Get a glove and give me a hand."

* * *

Metkovich was seldom called by his first name—George. Instead, he was known throughout the league as "Catfish." That label resulted from an incident that occurred a few years before he donned a Pirates uniform.

While trying out for the Boston Braves during spring training of 1942, Metkovich had taken advantage of an off day to go fishing. As he tells it, that afternoon he caught a pretty good-sized catfish. He reeled the fish into his boat and placed his bare foot on top of the fish as he attempted to remove the hook. Suddenly, he yelled out in pain as the flopping fish managed to spear his foot. With his foot now bleeding from the cut, Metkovich rowed the boat toward shore as quickly as he could, limped to his car, and drove to the emergency room of a local hospital. A physician cleaned the wound of fish fins and sewed the cut, but the damage had been done. Metkovich was sent back to camp in crutches. His chance to make the team vanished.

Braves manager Casey Stengel was reported as saying, "Who woulda believed it? We have a first baseman who's been attacked by a $#@*&_^% catfish!"

# Billy Meyer

The dubious honor of managing the 1952 Pittsburgh Pirates belonged to Billy Meyer, as the team compiled the infamous record of 42 wins and 112 losses. Named "Manager of the Year" four years earlier for his wisdom while leading the Bucs to a fourth-place finish just two games behind the second-place Cardinals, Meyer knew that 1952 would be his final year at the helm. In his frustration toward the end of the miserable season, Meyer lashed out at his team during a closed-door meeting. Included in his tirade was a classic line that crystallized the state of baseball in Pittsburgh that season: "You clowns can go on *What's My Line* in full uniforms and still stump the panel."

\* \* \*

Manager Billy Meyer came to the Pirates in 1948. In his first year, the Pirates seemed to play better than they knew how. With newcomers such as Stan Rojek at shortstop and Danny Murtaugh at second, along with pitchers Bob Chesnes and Elmer Riddle, Meyer guided to a fourth-place finish a team that was expected to finish in the basement. The '48 Bucs ended the season just two games behind second-place St. Louis.

For his accomplishments, Meyer was named "Manager of the Year." Some newspaper writers went so far as to suggest that Billy Meyer's style of managing was much better than that of most everyone in baseball, including the already legendary Casey Stengel, whose Yankees finished in third place in the American League.

The next year, in spite of a league-leading 54 home runs by Ralph Kiner, the Pirates dropped to seventh place in the standings. Consequently, some of the same critics who praised Meyer the year before now panned him and questioned why he could not be as successful as Casey Stengel, whose Yankees had just won the World Series.

During the winter meetings when Meyer met Stengel, "The Ol' Professor," Stengel said, "Billy, what I can't understand is how I got so smart so fast, and you got so dumb."

# Danny Murtaugh

Manager Danny Murtaugh was responsible for establishing a Major League Baseball "first," although he was totally unaware of it until he read about it in the next morning's *Pittsburgh Post-Gazette*. It occurred on September 1, 1971, when, prior to the start of the game, he brought to the umpires standing at home plate his starting lineup:

Rennie Stennett—second base
Gene Clines—center field
Roberto Clemente—right field
Willie Stargell—left field
Manny Sanguillen—catcher
Dave Cash—third base
Al Oliver—first base
Jackie Hernandez—shortstop
Dock Ellis—pitcher

The Pirates won the game that night by a score of 10-7 over the Philadelphia Phillies. Of even greater significance, however, was the fact that, for the first time in Major League Baseball history, a team filled its lineup with all minority players.

Lest anyone suggest that Murtaugh or anyone else in the Pirates organization did this as a gimmick for some instant publicity, he should be reminded that the Pirates were in the thick of a

*Prior to the first game of the '60 World Series, Pirate
skipper Danny Murtaugh tells puzzled Yankee manager
Casey Stengel that the Bucs intend to be world champions.*

pennant race (that they eventually won); thus management would
never put in jeopardy a club's chances of winning a ballgame just
to establish a record.

When he saw members of the news media standing outside his
private clubhouse office following the game, Murtaugh may have
anticipated that at least one of them might be thinking otherwise.
Before any of the reporters asked a question, he quickly put to
rest any such suspicion. "I put the best nine athletes out there.
The best nine I put out there tonight happened to be black. No
big deal. Next question."

\* \* \*

Danny Murtaugh had a reputation, especially in his early days
in baseball, for demonstrating his Irish temper when things did

not go as he had hoped. He told one story about himself when he was playing minor-league ball in the early 1940s at Houston in the Texas League. During one contest, this native of Chester, Pennsylvania, was at bat with the bases loaded and two outs. On a three-two count, Murtaugh took a pitch that he thought was outside. The umpire had another opinion and barked out, "Strike three!"

Murtaugh turned around in anger and, as a show of disgust with the call, tossed his bat high into the air.

The umpire quickly took off his mask and yelled, "If that bat hits the ground, you're fined 20 dollars."

The young Murtaugh quickly dove toward the falling piece of ash and grabbed it a split second before it hit the dirt.

"I would have been in a heck of a lot of trouble had I not caught that bat," said Murtaugh. "There was no way I could have paid that fine; the night before a group of us went out to a big party, and I didn't have 20 bucks left in my wallet."

\* \* \*

As a result of his close relationship with general manager Joe L. Brown, Danny Murtaugh was called upon to manage the Bucs four times (1957-1964, 1967, 1970-1971, and 1973-1976). He guided the Pirates to world championships in 1960 and 1971, plus East Division titles in 1970, 1974, and 1975.

In spite of these impressive statistics, the jovial Irishman downplayed his importance in winning ballgames. One of his oft-repeated speeches to his teams was, "If you keep it close in the eighth inning, I'll lose it every time, so make sure we have a big lead by then."

# Fritz Ostermueller

Watching 40-year-old Frederick "Fritz" Ostermueller pitch during his stint with the Pirates from 1944-1948 was a rare treat. The veteran southpaw employed a unique wind-up. Before throwing a pitch, "Old Folks Ostie" swung his long arms in such a huge arc that both hands came close to touching the mound. He brought his arms high over his head, then let go of the pitch. The routine was entertaining, but also time-consuming.

On June 24, 1947, the Bucs hosted the Brooklyn Dodgers at Forbes Field. Playing first base for the Dodgers that evening was rookie Jackie Robinson—baseball's pioneer African-American big-leaguer. Robinson, a speed merchant, had led off the fifth inning with a single and advanced to third on two infield groundouts. With the runner on third and two outs, Ostermueller took his full motion before his third pitch to Brooklyn's Fred "Dixie" Walker.

Suddenly, just as the Pirates pitcher bent low to the ground, Robinson darted for home. Ostermueller seemed oblivious to his teammates, the coaches and the 35,331 partisan fans screaming for his attention. As it turned out, he was also unmindful of Robinson. By the time he brought his arms over his head, Ostermueller saw Robinson slide across the plate in front of catcher Homer "Dixie" Howell.

All Ostermueller could do was stand on the hill with the look of utter frustration. Following the 4-2 loss to the Dodgers that evening, the veteran Ostermueller attempted to justify his performance. "Nobody could have predicted he [Robinson] would do a foolish thing like that."

The record books show that Jackie Robinson would "do that foolish thing" a total of 19 times during his 10-year career in Major League Baseball.

# Jim Pagliaroni

A familiar sight at the annual winter gatherings known as "PirateFests" is former catcher Jim Pagliaroni, who played with the Bucs from 1963-1967. Fans today appreciate the opportunity to meet him and to get a treasured autograph. However, not all of his guest appearances have received standing ovations.

Shortly after he and pitcher Don Schwall came to the Bucs from the Boston Red Sox in a trade for Dick Stuart and Jack Lamabe, Pittsburgh was playing the Mets at the Polo Grounds. The Pirates beat New York that day, and as was customary, one or two players from the winning team were invited to appear as guests with Mets announcer Ralph Kiner on his postgame televised show, *Kiner's Korner.* Arranging for Pagliaroni and Schwall to be interviewed was Pirate broadcaster Bob Prince, a close friend of Kiner, a former Bucs superstar.

Instead of appearing on camera in their baseball uniforms, as was the custom for most players, Pagliaroni and Schwall wrapped themselves in bed sheets that had now become togas, combed their hair down over their foreheads, grabbed some bunches of grapes from the player's buffet and talked with lisps.

Kiner sat stunned. Whenever the former Pirates slugger asked any question, either Pagliaroni or Schwall would smack lips, hold out limp wrists and wink at their host. No matter what Kiner attempted to do, he could not get a serious response from either man. He struggled the best he could to make the most of the situation. Nothing worked.

Following the abbreviated telecast (cut short because of the antics of the two guests), Pirate general manager Joe L. Brown was angry that two of his players would pull such a trick. Bob Prince, Jim Pagliaroni, Don Schwall and every viewer who saw the show thought it was side-splitting.

All Ralph Kiner would say was, "No comment."

# Dave Parker

One of the more talented players in Pirate history was Dave "The Cobra" Parker. The 6'5" left-handed-hitting outfielder had power, speed and a strong arm. He presented a frightening picture at the plate for any opposing pitcher.

When Parker announced his plans to become a vegetarian, his teammate, pitcher John Candelaria, asked, "What are you going to eat? Redwoods?"

\* \* \*

Veteran shortstop Dal Maxvill was with the Bucs briefly during the 1973-74 seasons. In mid-July 1973, when the 6'5", 230-pound rookie Parker walked onto the field wearing his brand new Pirates uniform, Maxvill turned to one of his teammates and said, "I don't know who this guy is, but I'm glad he's on our side!"

\* \* \*

Dave Parker had perhaps as much raw talent as anyone who donned the black and gold of the Pittsburgh Pirates. As a member of the heralded "Lumber Company" in the 1970s, Parker won

*Dave Parker: "The Cobra"*

consecutive batting titles in 1977 and 1978. He earned the coveted Most Valuable Player Award in '78.

Nobody could argue the fact that he possessed enormous power at the plate and could run like the wind. Even more amazing was his throwing arm. In one All-Star Game (1979), Parker exhibited this superb skill to a national television audience when he threw out not just one, but two base runners who attempted to take extra bases.

Parker, however, was one of those superstars who became his own worst enemy. While most of us are taught from childhood how to be gracious losers, Parker was among those who never learned how to be a gracious winner.

When the Pirates made him the game's first million-dollar-a-year position player with a $7.9 million, five-year deal in 1979, at a time when Pittsburgh was suffering from the economic woes of a declining steel industry and rising unemployment, Parker did nothing to enhance his image when he spent bundles of money on expensive gold chains to wear around his neck during the game. One of those chains included a diamond-studded pendant that spelled out "C O B R A"—Parker's nickname. Another time he wore a huge Star of David, because, as he told the news media, "My name is David and I'm a star." Much to the dismay of fans, he also sported an earring.

Citizens in other cities around the nation may have accepted this fashion statement, but not Pittsburghers. Fathers and mothers with the so-called "steel-mill mentality" and an unmistakably traditional set of values, objected to paying high prices for admission to take their children to ballgames, only to see someone they deemed to be an overpaid and cocky ballplayer who seemed to delight in flaunting his newfound wealth. Unfortunately, a few of the fans became even more incensed because Parker was a minority. When Parker refused to sign autographs for kids prior to the start of a game, that was all the Bucs fans needed. Most of them openly rebelled against him.

In one dark moment in the life of Parker and of the Pirates, an irate fan threw at him a battery from a transistor radio. The flying missile missed Parker's head by inches. Had it struck him, it could have resulted in serious injury. For his own protection, he was escorted off the field by manager Chuck Tanner.

Parker's days were numbered with Pittsburgh. In 1984, he moved to Cincinnati as a free agent.

A few years later, Parker confessed to police investigators that he and others on the Pirates were involved with using cocaine. It was a national scandal that hurt Parker, Pittsburgh and Major League Baseball.

It's one tale from the Pittsburgh Pirates dugout that everyone would rather forget. At the same time, we dare not.

# Deacon Phillippe

In 1903, the Pirates, led by star players such as Fred Clarke, Tommy Leach and Honus Wagner, won their third consecutive National League pennant. Only this time, the season was not yet over. Owner Barney Dreyfuss and his Pirates agreed to play the number-one team of the upstart American League for a best-of-nine "Championship Series" (it would later be called the "World Series").

Baseball insiders of the era considered the American League little more than a "minor league." Nevertheless, the Pirates agreed to play the Series against the Boston Pilgrims (now the Red Sox).

A most effective pitcher for the Bucs that year was Charles "Deacon" Phillippe (24-7), who pitched the opening game and won against the legendary Denton "Cy" Young by a score of 7-3. The Baptist Sunday school teacher (hence his nickname) in his home town of Rural Retreat, Virginia, also won Games 3 and 4. After Boston tied the Series three games apiece, Phillippe pitched and lost the next game by a 7-3 score. Following a one-day rain delay, the "Deacon" was sent to the mound for a record fifth start in one Series. Boston blanked the Pirates 3-0 to win baseball's first postseason Series, five games to three.

It was a humiliating loss for the Pirates and for the National League. In fact, the next year's National League Champs—the New York Giants—refused to play Boston. Giants manager John McGraw said that he would not be dragged into a contest with "minor-leaguers."

# Bob Prince

Like his predecessor, Rosey Rowswell, the Bucs' announcer Bob Prince coined his own unique phrases as he described the action on the field. When one of the Pirates hit a home run, for instance, Prince shouted, "You can kiss it good-bye!" A Pirates hit between the outfielders was a "tweener." A "bug on the rug" was a Pirates hit that bounced on the artificial turf of Three Rivers Stadium, out of the reach of opposing outfielders. When a relief pitcher entered the game with runners on base, Prince called for a "Hoover" or a "vacuum"—his designation for a double-play ground ball.

If a Pirate pitcher just missed nicking the corner of home plate, Prince described it as being off by "a gnat's eyelash." When Roberto Clemente made one of his circus catches or would throw out a runner with a strong throw from the outfield, Prince intoned: "Bobbyyyyyy Clemente!" When the Pirates wrapped up a victory, he exclaimed with gusto, "How sweet it is!"—a phrase borrowed later by comedian Jackie Gleason. Finally, whenever the Bucs were able to squeak out a victory with a last-inning run, Prince sighed with an aura of satirical confidence, "We had 'em all the way."

\* \* \*

Bob Prince was not above anything in an attempt to generate fan excitement. During the 1966 season, for example, Prince devised a method of snuffing out an opposing team's rally. From the broadcast booth, he "placed a curse" on the visiting team by sticking out an eight-foot-long piece of cardboard shaped like a hot dog. It didn't look like a typical hot dog. It was painted a bright, Kelly green. Fans and media called it "The Green Weenie."

During the home games, when the opposition began to amass some hits, fans faced the KDKA booth and hollered, "Hey, Bob. Get out the Green Weenie!" When Prince responded, the crowd let out a hearty cheer.

Even a first-year student of logic understands that there is no correlation whatsoever between the sudden appearance of such a gimmick and a change of luck on the field. But perhaps due to the opposing players being "psyched out" by this phenomenon, the "curse of the Green Weenie" seemed to work.

A *Time* magazine story about the contending Pirates that year featured two photos—a group picture of the team and, of course, of Bob Prince demonstrating the proper use of the now legendary "Green Weenie."

\* \* \*

Those who listened to Bob Prince during his tenure as voice of the Pirates quickly realized that this flamboyant man was a "homer"—i.e., someone who openly rooted for his team. "Calling a game with cold dispassion is a cinch," he often said. "You sit on your can, reporting grounders and two-base hits lackadaisically. You've got no responsibilities. But rooting is tough. It requires creativeness. It also fulfills your function, which is to shill. You are the arm of the home club who is there to make the listener happy."

\* \* \*

One of Bob Prince's trademarks was his rather outlandish apparel. "You could see his flashy sport coats coming from ten blocks away," said veteran Boston Red Sox (and later NBC-TV) announcer Curt Gowdy.

Prince was never shy about creating his own fashion statement when he wore $500 Gucci shoes . . . and no socks. When questioned about this, Prince answered with a flip, "It's gauche to wear socks with Gucci."

\* \* \*

Bob "The Gunner" Prince was a boy in a man's body. At times, this became most apparent to those closest to him. During a road trip in 1959, for example, Prince bet Pirates slugger Dick Stuart that he could jump from a third-story window at the Chase Hotel in St. Louis into the hotel's swimming pool. What Stuart didn't know was that Prince was a varsity diver on his high school and college teams. Nonetheless, there was a distance of eight feet between the wall of the hotel and the edge of the pool. Prince's former broadcasting sidekick Nellie King recalled, "It was a hellava dangerous jump. It was a kinda crazy thing to do."

Prince stood on the ledge of a window three flights up, bent his legs and sprang high into the air. He cleared the edge of the pool by just a couple of inches. When he came up to the surface of the pool, he shook his head from side to side, spraying water from his hair and exclaimed, "We had 'em all the way."

Did Bob Prince ever regret performing this perilous feat? "Yeah," answered The Gunner, "but not because I jumped. I was ticked off 'cause Stuart never paid up on the lousy 20 bucks he owed me."

\* \* \*

Bob Prince was never shy about giving players nicknames. He baptized pitcher Ron Kline, for example, as "The Callery, PA, Hummer," since the hard-throwing right-hander hailed from that city in nearby Butler County. He bestowed upon third baseman Don Hoak the name "Tiger" and dubbed outfielder Dave Parker the "Cobra" because of his coiled batting stance. And Prince, because of his close friendship with "The Great One," was perhaps the only person on this planet who could refer to Roberto Clemente as "Bobby."

Prince, too, had a nickname. They called him "The Gunner." As to why he was called this depends on what story you believe. One reason for the designation is because of his rapid-fire delivery. The second is because of the widespread rumor that he was at a local tavern talking with some attentive young woman when her husband burst into the establishment while carrying a shotgun. He pointed the weapon at Prince and threatened to shoot him. Prince, however, was able to talk his way out of the situation, and all those involved quietly left the premises without anyone getting hurt.

* * *

Bob Prince believed in the economy of words. Certainly, he was a glib conversationalist who liked to spin yarns and trade anecdotes with friends and fans, but when it was appropriate, during a broadcast he allowed the silence of the moment to make a statement.

This became abundantly clear one evening during the 1961 season when the Bucs were playing a night game in St. Louis. The Pirates were leading the Cardinals by a score of 4-3. St. Louis had a runner on first with two outs in the bottom of the ninth. Up to the plate strode Stan "The Man" Musial.

This native of Donora, Pennsylvania, had always been hard on the Pirates. One might think that he piled up those terrific offensive numbers just to remind the Bucs about the horrible mistake in judgment they made when they refused to sign him as a teenage southpaw pitcher in 1938.

Prince reminded his listening audience, as he did so often, about the situation on the field at that moment. Just one out separated his beloved Bucs from a victory. He described Musial's unorthodox stance at the plate—holding his bat high, perpendicular to the ground. He bent his body in such a way that he resembled a man peeking at the pitcher from around a corner.

Prince described the action: "Saint Louis Cardinal fans are murmuring with excitement. Earl Francis stares into his catcher Smoky Burgess. Musial stands and waits. Francis goes into his stretch. He kicks. He delivers."

The radio audience suddenly heard a loud *crack*—the unmistakable sound of a bat squarely hitting a baseball—immediately followed by a robust cheer from the partisan Cardinal fans.

Prince sat quiet in front of the open microphone for ten full seconds, then said: "We'll be back in a moment with a wrapup of tonight's game."

No declaration that a home run had been hit. No mention that the Pirates had lost the contest. No reference to a bad pitch. No comment on anything whatsoever. "We'll be back in a moment. . ."

That said it all.

# Dino Restelli

Pittsburgh-born artist Andy Warhol is credited with observing, "The day will come when everyone will be famous for 15 minutes." When he said this, he may have had someone like Dino Restelli in mind.

No description of the Pirates' 1949 season would be complete without a reference to Dino Restelli. Brought up from the San Francisco Seals in midseason, this powerfully built Italian American became an overnight sensation. In his first two weeks in the majors, Restelli slammed nine home runs.

Adding to his charisma was some "down-home color." He carried a large, red handkerchief that he often pulled from his hip pocket to wipe his brow and clean the thick eyeglasses that also became a trademark. The impact on baseball from this naïve rookie from the back streets of St. Louis capturing the hearts of fans everywhere was the subject of a cover story in *Life* magazine.

Batting ahead of perennial home run champion Ralph Kiner, he became part of a "one-two punch" that was the topic of conversation around the league. Restelli, it seemed, could hit any pitcher's fastball out of the park.

Unfortunately for Restelli and the Pittsburgh Baseball Club, it was the curveball that gave him problems—something opposing pitchers soon discovered. As a result, he hit only three more

*Dino Restelli was living proof that Andy Warhol was correct.*

homers during the remainder of the '49 campaign and finished with a .250 batting average.

Those 15 minutes ticked away quickly. Following spring training the next year, Dino Restelli's name did not appear on the team roster.

# Branch Rickey

Commenting on the dismal season of the 1952 Pirates when they ended the year in last place with a 42-112 record, executive vice president and general manager Branch Rickey was quoted as saying, "They finished last—on merit."

\* \* \*

"It's easy to figure out Mr. Rickey's thinking about contracts. He had both players and money—and just didn't like to see the two of them mix."
—Chuck Connors, former major-leaguer turned actor.

\* \* \*

When evaluating potential big-league ballplayers, Mr. Rickey believed in bringing every willing candidate into a tryout camp. His philosophy was to sign hundreds of cheaply paid prospects with the hope that at least a few of them would work out. "If you scoop up enough talent," he said, "you can develop quality out of quantity."

In spite of this philosophy, there were two kinds of athletes in which the Bible-quoting, tee-totaling lawyer known as "Mahatma"

*Paul Pettit—the "bonus baby." It looks here like he pitched while wearing a batting helmet. Was this the reason he failed to win in the big leagues?*

had absolutely no interest. He explained, "I would never sign a medical student; he's already dedicated to another vocation. And never sign a divinity student; the world's in bad enough shape that we don't want to take anyone away from the Lord's work."

\* \* \*

Branch Rickey left the Brooklyn Dodgers in 1949 to reorganize the Pittsburgh Pirates. Although he brought with him three of his favorite scouts, Howie Haak, Clyde Sukeforth and Rex Bowen, Rickey felt that this was one team he could not build from the bottom up; he lacked sufficient time and money. Yielding, perhaps, to pressure from the media and the fans to turn things around instantly, Rickey tried for a quick fix by entering the bonus market. His efforts fell flat.

In 1950, for example, he gave $100,000 to a Los Angeles high-school southpaw named Paul Pettit. The youngster won only one game in the major leagues. By 1954, Mr. Rickey had been burned so often by other deals that had gone south, he decided not to give a bonus of $10,000 to another lefty—this one from New York. Instead, he called his former team, the Dodgers, suggesting that they might want to take a chance on the kid.

Mr. Rickey should have spent the money. The youngster's name was Sandy Koufax.

# Curt Roberts

On Opening Day, April 13, 1954, the starting second baseman was a rookie named Curtis Benjamin Roberts—the first
African American to play for the Pirates. In a 4-2 victory over
the Phillies, Roberts hit a triple in three at-bats at Forbes Field.

This was seven years after Jackie Robinson broke the color
barrier in Major League Baseball. Roberts, therefore, did not suf-
fer quite as many slings and arrows of prejudice as did those who
blazed the trail before him. One of his fellow rookie teammates,
pitcher Nellie King, recalled, "We didn't think of him as a black
guy. He was just a player. He could be a pain in the ass at times
and a real nice kid at times, just like anyone else."

Curt Roberts's career covered only three seasons, all with
Pittsburgh. He knew his chances for any future with the club were
slim when, in 1956, he was replaced by another second baseman,
a rookie named Mazeroski.

# Bob Robertson

First sacker Bob Robertson was a fixture for the '71 Bucs. Although he batted a respectable .271 and slammed 26 home runs that year, he played in the shadow of two of the game's established superstars—Willie Stargell and Roberto Clemente. However, in Game 3 of the World Series that year, his own star shone because of a blunder.

With the Pirates ahead by a score of 2-1 in the bottom half of the seventh inning and no outs, Clemente and Stargell had reached base safely. As Robertson approached the batter's box, manager Danny Murtaugh flashed the sign to third base coach Frank Oceak for a sacrifice bunt; Oceak relayed it to Robinson. With runners on first and second and nobody out, this was the obvious call. Baltimore's manager, Earl Weaver, knew this. The pitcher, Pat Dobson, knew this. Both Clemente and Stargell knew this. In fact, everybody in Three Rivers Stadium seemed to know this except for one person—Bob Robertson.

Robertson somehow missed the sign. "I don't know if I had seen Oceak, to be honest with you," recalls Robertson. "I was so focused on that I was going to do. I certainly was not looking for a bunt sign. I don't know if I ever did bunt in the big leagues."

The instant Dobson released the pitch, third baseman Brooks Robinson and first baseman "Boog" Powell rushed toward the plate to field the anticipated bunt. Robertson, however, didn't bunt. Instead, he took a mighty swing. Both fielders fell to the ground to avoid being hit by a potential line drive. That proved to be unnecessary. The ball was hit far over their heads; in fact, it sailed deep into the right center field stands for a three-run homer.

Robertson circled the bases and crossed home plate with the run that sealed a 5-1 victory. Waiting to greet him was teammate Willie Stargell, who shook his hand and exclaimed, "Nice bunt."

# Jim Rooker

Sometimes it's better just to *think* about what you might do instead of *saying* it for all the world to hear. Pirate broadcaster Jim Rooker may not have said something heard by everyone on this planet, but speaking before the thousands who listened on the Pittsburgh Pirates Radio Network was enough to cause him aches and humiliation.

On June 8, 1989, the Bucs had forged ahead with a 10-run first-inning uprising against the Philadelphia Phils in Veterans Stadium, highlighted by a three-run shot into the stands by outfielder Barry Bonds. Rooker, a former pitcher for the Bucs who was one of the main cogs of a team that won the 1979 World Series against Baltimore, was a sidekick to Lanny Frattare from 1981-1993. But no amount of broadcast experience could have prepared him for what was undoubtedly his most regrettable pronouncement.

Since 10 Pirates runners had crossed the plate even before the Phillies got their first at-bat, an overconfident Jim Rooker openly declared, "If the Pirates lose this one, I'll *walk* back to Pittsburgh."

As if they were following a script written for a "B" movie, the Phils pecked away. One of the unlikely heroes was shortstop Steve Jeltz (only four homers all year), who hit a two-run homer and a three-run blast. Joining him in the hit parade were legitimate power hitters Von Hayes, who hit another pair of two-run shots, and Darren Daulton, who smacked a two-run single in the eighth inning to break an 11-11 tie. The Pirates never recovered and eventually lost the game.

Following the loss, Pirate relief pitcher Jeff Robinson, who had allowed four runs in just one-third of an inning, moaned, "It couldn't get any worse than that." Perhaps not for him, but it did for Rooker. He had made a promise; now he had to deliver.

During the off season, Rooker, indeed, made his unintentional walk, hoofing it all 305 miles from Philadelphia to Pittsburgh. But some good came out of this experience. After the 13-day trek, as he was soaking his blistered feet, Rooker counted the donations for charity given by supportive fans. They totaled more than $81,000.

# Rosey Rowswell

Albert K. "Rosey" Rowswell had a unique way of describing a baseball game. The blatantly partisan 5'6", 120-pounder coined a lingo that became familiar to Pirates listeners of the games he broadcast on WWSW and KDKA radio. He described the strike-out of an opposing batter, for example, as the "old dipsy doodle." If a Pirate slapped an extra-base hit, it was a "doozey marooney." When Pittsburgh was able to load the bases, he remarked, "They're F.O.B. (Full of Bucs)." If the opposition put on a hitting display (as it did many times during his broadcasting career from 1936-1954), Rowswell moaned, "Oh, my achin' back."

Perhaps the most famous of all Rowswell's calls was when a Pirate smacked a home run. In lieu of a simple "It's outta here," "Going . . . going . . . gone," or some trite statement, Rowswell called upon a mythical relative when he shouted, "Raise the window, Aunt Minnie. Here she comes—right into your petunia patch!"

During the away games, Rowswell refused to leave home. As a result, he and his sidekick—the flashy Bob Prince—recreated the games from a local studio. From the ballpark, brief messages were sent via a Western Union relay setup. The announcers called

*Aunt Minnie's favorite nephew—Rosey Rowswell—shows young Bob Prince some of the secrets to success in describing Pirate baseball games.*

the play-by-play based on terse announcements such as "Westlake flies out to right," then added a basketful of imagination.

Rowswell's description of a home run included his patented "Raise the window, Aunt Minnie" call. On these occasions, while standing in front of the microphone, Prince dropped onto a table a tray piled with nuts, bolts, tin cans, or anything else that simulated the sound of breaking glass. Rowswell then sighed, "She never made it. She never made it."

* * *

Rosey Rowswell was a popular after-dinner speaker. Following his inspirational talks that were enhanced by his own poems and selected anecdotes, he usually concluded the evening with an opportunity for members of the audience to raise questions.

After one of Rowswell's speeches at a father-son banquet in Bower Hill, a 12-year-old youngster in the crowd asked, "Mr. Rowswell, what does it take to become a big-league baseball announcer?"

Rosey probably heard that question a hundred times before, but he answered it as though he was answering the inquiry for the first time. The diminutive broadcaster stood erect and gazed directly in the eye of the questioner. In a tone reminiscent of a wise philosopher he said, "The best advice I can give is this: As soon as you get home, find that little bag in which you keep marbles. Then, stuff as many marbles into your mouth as you can. Once your mouth is full, stand in front of a mirror and practice speaking. Then take out the marbles one at a time, while you are still speaking. Once you have lost all of your marbles, you are now ready to become a baseball announcer."

That was just a sample of the wit and wisdom of Rosey Rowswell. Pittsburgh was blessed to have him as part of its family.

\* \* \*

"To the hundreds of thousands of district baseball fans, Rosey Rowswell was the symbol of the Pirates."

—*Pittsburgh Press* reporting the death of Aunt Minnie's favorite nephew on February 6, 1955.

# Babe Ruth

Perhaps the most memorable moment in 1935 for the Pirates came not from one wearing the black and gold of the Bucs. Instead, it came from the bat of an old American League hero who now wore the uniform of the National League's Boston Braves. George Herman "Babe" Ruth had signed a contract with the Braves as a part-time player and club vice president.

Ruth was not a content player. He thought he was brought into the Braves' organization to become an executive or as a future team manager. Not so. The Braves wanted him only as a drawing card for fans. Babe Ruth now knew this.

He also knew that his best days were far behind him. He was woefully out of shape, and his batting average had dipped to a puny .181 in the 28 games he had played that year. On this particular May 25, however, the 41-year-old legend left for the baseball world one more glorious moment.

During his first three times at bat in Forbes Field that afternoon, he smacked three home runs—the last one was off a pretty good pitcher for the Bucs, Guy Bush. To the astonishment of both the players and the fans, the towering blast cleared the roof above the right field stands. It seemed that only gravity kept the ball on this planet. Babe Ruth became the first player ever to smack a ball over the 86-foot-high right field stands.

Bush recalled the homer. "I never saw a ball hit so hard. He was fat and old, but he still had that great swing. Even when he missed, you could hear the bat go *swishhhhh!* I can never forget that last home run he hit off me. It's probably still going."

On his last at-bat that day, Ruth singled to right. As he stood on first base, the "Sultan of Swat" called time out and took himself out of the game. As he walked to the Braves dugout, he tipped his hat to an appreciative crowd of about 10,000 applauding Pittsburgh fans who had just seen him hit the last home run—number 714—of his fabled career.

A few days later, a sad, bitter George Herman Ruth officially retired from the game of baseball.

# Manny Sanguillen

One of the most popular (and talented) Pirate players ever to don a catcher's mask was Manuel De Jesus "Manny" Sanguillen. Years before he opened his famous barbecue stand at PNC Park, this native Panamanian was an effective handler of pitchers and was also quite good with the stick. One thing that Sanguillen lacked, however, was patience in the batter's box. During his 12 years with the Pirates (1967-1976, 1978-1980), he seldom received a base on balls; instead, in his eagerness to get hits, he swung at anything near the plate. General manager Joe L. Brown once quipped, "When Manny takes a pitch, either it's a wild pitch or paralysis has set in."

*Manny Sanguillen loved to hit. He hated to walk.*

# Rip Sewell

Right-handed pitcher Truett Banks "Rip" Sewell was a main-stay with the Pirates for 12 of his 13 big-league years. After leading the National League with 21 victories in 1943, he duplicated the number of wins the following season. Only now, he added another pitch to his arsenal—a blooper that he tossed 20 to 25 feet into the air. Hitters, often not knowing what they were seeing come at them, had a difficult time connecting with a ball that seemed to float up to the plate.

One of Sewell's teammates—outfielder Maurice Van Robays—dubbed it an "eephus pitch." He explained, "An eephus ain't nothin', and that's what the ball is."

\* \* \*

Rip Sewell used to claim that nobody ever hit his famous blooper pitch for a home run. Not so. In the 1946 All-Star Game played at Fenway Park in Boston, local hero Ted Williams faced Sewell in the eighth inning. When he stepped into the batter's box, Williams yelled out to Sewell, "You're not going to throw me that *#%@*^ pitch in an All-Star Game, are you?" Sewell didn't answer. He just stared at Williams and flashed an impish grin.

If Williams had any doubts about the answer to his question, he only had to watch the first pitch—a classic "eephus" that headed for the middle of the strike zone. Williams swung and sent the ball screaming foul, deep into the stands above first base. The second pitch, a rare fastball, was a strike. The third, another blooper, resembled an underhand toss by a corporate accountant at a company picnic. Williams stepped forward a full stride, swung his 40-inch bat, and sent the ball high over the fence in right field for a home run. As Williams circled the bases to the cheers of the Boston faithful, both he and Sewell grinned broadly at each other.

Later, Williams claimed that, had he done this in a regular ballgame, he would have been called out; when he hit the ball, he was more than two feet out of the batter's box.

What was Sewell's rationale for claiming that his blooper had never been hit for a home run? Sewell answered that question with a well-publicized response: "Bah! That pitch wasn't high enough to be a *real* blooper."

\* \* \*

During the 1947 season, Pittsburgh, in fact, had two "senior citizens" on its roster. Both Rip Sewell and Fritz Ostermueller were 40-year-olds. Ostermueller would pitch for one more season; Sewell actually pitched two more years.

Because of his advancing age, Sewell was retired from the Bucs staff and named as a Pirates coach prior to the '49 campaign. However, while watching him instruct young hurlers during spring training in Fort Myers, Florida, manager Billy Meyer became convinced that Sewell showed more "stuff" than the remainder of his pitching staff. Two days before the Pirates broke camp and headed north, Meyer removed Sewell's name from his coaching staff and added it to the regular roster. Sewell, in fact, was named the starting pitcher for the home opener, and he beat the Cubs 1-0. He finished that year (his last) with a 6-1 record.

\* \* \*

Rip Sewell was not always a favorite teammate among those who were sympathetic toward a new (some would say heretical) movement in Major League Baseball. In 1946, a man named Robert Murphy attempted to form what he called the American Baseball Guild—a union for players in the major leagues. Since Pittsburgh was a strong union city, Murphy believed that the Pirates would the easiest team to support his cause.

Sewell, however, became a big stumbling block for Murphy's quest. The big right-hander felt that unions would be the "death" of Major League Baseball as he knew it, and he openly spoke out against the union. His words were most effective in combating the drive. By a slim majority, Pirate players voted against joining the union; thus the efforts of Mr. Murphy and his crew went for naught.

Murphy later complained that had Sewell not "kissed up so much to management, the union vote would have turned out differently."

Prior to the start of home opener of the '47 season, baseball commissioner A.B. "Happy" Chandler presented a watch to Sewell in appreciation of his pro-management stance. This ceremony did nothing to help settle the lingering tensions in the clubhouse between the pro-union and pro-management forces.

\* \* \*

Rip Sewell spent his last years in the little town of Plant City, Florida. In spite of the fact that he had lost both legs due to diabetes, he played a mean game of golf every chance he could get. During his conversations with former teammates and fans, he was never shy about comparing modern-day players with those of his generation.

"First the players wanted a hamburger, and the owners give them a hamburger. Then they wanted filet mignon, and they give them a filet mignon. Then they wanted the whole damn cow, and now that they got the cow, they want a pasture to put her in. You can't satisfy 'em, and I have no sympathy for any of 'em."

# Hal Smith

Game 7 of the 1960 World Series will always be remembered by Pirate faithful as perhaps the greatest moment in Bucs history—perhaps in all of baseball. The experts did not give the Pirates a chance against a potent New York Yankees lineup filled with household names—Mickey Mantle, Roger Maris, Yogi Berra and the like. Yet the Bucs won the final game of the Series in dramatic fashion with a ninth-inning blast by future Hall of Famer Bill Mazeroski.

The opportunity for Maz to have his name forever etched in the minds and hearts of every Pittsburgher came in the home half of the eighth inning with the Yankees leading by a score of 7-5. With the Bucs' Gino Cimoli on first and nobody out, Bill Virdon hit a sharp grounder to short. The ball took a weird bounce and struck Tony Kubek in the throat, knocking the Yankee shortstop out of the game.

"Maybe God could have done something about that play; man could not," moaned Yankee manager Casey Stengel. Whatever the reason, both runners were safe.

Dick Groat followed with a single, scoring Cimoli. The Bucs were now only one run down, and the capacity crowd cheered with hope for a miracle.

The cheering fans fell silent when Rocky Nelson flied out. But Roberto Clemente brought them back to life when he tapped an

*Hal Smith hit "the most underrated home run in*
*baseball history" during the final game of the '60 World Series.*

infield chopper toward the right side of the diamond and, running like the wind, barely beat a throw to first. The cheers increased in volume when reserve catcher Hal Smith stepped to the plate.

Smith, a. 295 hitter, with 11 homers that year, had some power. The fans hoped, even prayed, for anything. The gods of baseball (at least those of Pirate baseball) must have been listening. Smith swung and sent a line drive deep over the left field wall, giving the Bucs a 9-7 lead.

The Yankees tied the game in the top of the ninth; that set the stage for the oft-repeated story about the homer by Maz.

None of this, however, would have been possible had it not been for the home run hit by the unsung hero of the Series— Harold Wayne Smith.

\* \* \*

"Hal Smith's home run in the seventh game of the World Series is the most underrated homer in baseball history."
    —Dick Groat, shortstop and team captain, 1960 Pirates.

* * *

"Pittsburgh has just become an insane asylum. We have seen and shared in one of baseball's great moments."
    —Broadcaster Chuck Thompson after Hal Smith's home run in Game 7 of the 1960 World Series.

# Willie Stargell

The most respected leader of the Pirates as they surged toward winning the pennant in 1979 was Wilver Dornel "Willie" Stargell. Teammates affectionately called him "Pops." He became the solidifying element for the entire Pirate family both on and off the field. Teammate Tim Foli once observed, "When Willie walks into the clubhouse, everyone stops talking and waits for him to let us know what he plans for that day."

\* \* \*

Willie Stargell was always eager to praise individual performance of his teammates. During the '79 campaign, he dispensed "Stargell Stars" to those who made exceptional plays or timely hits. The players wore them with pride on their caps.

Today, around the base of his statue outside PNC Park, are stars representing those coveted "Stargell Stars."

\* \* \*

The Pirates' manager from 1977-1985 was Chuck Tanner. Nobody better than he realized the importance of clubhouse leadership such as the kind "Pops" brought to the team. "Hav-

*Hall of Famer Willie "Pops" Stargell was a welcomed
addition to the announcer's booth for nationally televised games.*

ing Willie Stargell on your club is like having a diamond ring on
your finger," he said.

Outsiders, too, recognized this intangible trait of the one so
dearly loved by both the fans and his teammates. Robin Roberts,

former pitching great for the Phillies, said, "I think if you have a leader like a Willie Stargell on your team, you're all right."

\* \* \*

Although he struck fear into the hearts of opposing pitchers when this 6'2", 188-pound mass of solid muscle would swing his bat in circles as though it were a toothpick, Willie Stargell continually had trouble trying to hit against three pitchers—Bob Gibson, Steve Carlton and Sandy Koufax. Stargell used this analogy: "Hitting against them is like drinking coffee with a fork."

# Dick Stuart

In 1956, two years prior to his rookie season in the majors, big (6'4", 212 pounds) Dick Stuart set a minor-league record by clobbering 66 home runs for a Class A team in Lincoln, Nebraska. He showed the same tape-measure power during his stay in Pittsburgh from 1958-1962 and with five other teams before he ended his 10-year career. He was, for example, the first batter ever to hit a ball over the old "iron gates" in Forbes Field—408 feet away from home plate.

Power hitting was his forte; fielding was not. For seven consecutive years, Stuart either tied or led the majors in errors for a first baseman.

The media tagged him with less than complimentary nicknames, including "Dr. Strangeglove," "Stonefingers," and "Clank."

Once, when the public address announcer, Art McKennan, warned fans that "Anyone who interferes with the ball in play will be ejected from the ballpark," Pirate manager Danny Murtaugh responded, "I hope Stuart doesn't think that means him."

Stuart himself made light of this when he ordered a special vanity plate for his automobile that read "E-3."

\* \* \*

*In the late '50s, Dick Stuart, Dale Long and
Frank Thomas led the Pirates' "hit parade."*

Stuart, who passed away in December 2002, often told this
self-deprecating story about his lack of fielding prowess.

"One night in Pittsburgh, the wind was blowing exceptionally
hard, and pieces of paper were flying around the field. I happened
to see a hot-dog wrapper fly by. I reached out, grabbed it on the
fly and stuffed it into my pocket. Immediately, 30,000 fans gave
me a standing ovation."

\* \* \*

Dick Stuart knew his limitations. He was the first to admit that he was never a candidate for a Gold Glove Award. Yet that fact never bothered him. "I knew I was close to being the world's worst fielder, but who gets paid for fielding?" asked the slugging first baseman who, after retirement, worked in California as a bill collector. "There wasn't a great fielder in baseball getting the kind of dough I got for hitting."

\* \* \*

During one of his after-dinner speeches, Dick Stuart introduced his wife to an audience of aware baseball fans. "Behind every successful man is a good woman," said the slugger.

"Yeah," answered a fan in the crowd, "and she had better be wearing a first baseman's mitt."

\* \* \*

To be charitable, let's say that Dick Stuart was a free spirit. He did not enjoy being governed by rules and regulations. This fun-loving first baseman also was among the first to turn a potential confrontation into a laugh with one well-placed quip. In short, Stuart believed that life was to be enjoyed to the fullest without limitations. He sometimes carried that philosophy onto the ball field.

Manager Danny Murtaugh was a patient man who could put up with an occasional display of independence as long as his club was winning. At the same time, he was quick to pull in the reins whenever his team was on a losing streak.

During one such stretch during the 1962 campaign, Stuart had either missed a sign or had taken it upon himself to disobey the sign; nobody knows for sure. After the game, Murtaugh brought Stuart into his office and lambasted him: "Remember, Stuart, when it comes to calling the shots around here, I'm the manager, and you're nothin'."

Stuart nodded and turned to leave the office. But Murtaugh wanted to be certain that Stuart knew the rules. "Did you get the message?" shouted the manager, his Irish face now red with anger.

"Yeah," replied Stuart before opening the door. "You're the manager of nothin'."

Murtaugh, for one of the rare moments in his career, resigned himself to silence.

# Billy Sunday

Once upon a time, a preacher played right field for Pittsburgh. Prior to the 1888 season, the Pittsburgh "Alleghenies" (the name of the team in that era) purchased from the Chicago White Stockings (forerunner of the Cubs) a fleet-footed, .248-hitting outfielder. His name was William Ashley Sunday. "Billy" Sunday played with Pittsburgh until 1890 when he was traded to the Phillies.

His real claim to fame came several years later, not on the grass of a baseball diamond, but on sawdust-covered aisles between rows of rented chairs inside a canvas tent. When he "found religion" and became one of the nation's most famous evangelists, he drew thousands to his revivals held across the country.

Often Billy Sunday peppered his fiery sermons with illustrations learned in his days on a baseball diamond, such as the times, according to one reporter, he would run across the stage in front of worshippers, and "slide into God's home plate while shouting out, "Safe!"" much to the delight of the crowd.

Sunday also wowed audiences with his emotional attacks on the evils of alcohol. He promised to punch, kick and bite the plague of demon rum. "And when I'm old, and toothless, and fistless, and footless, I'll gum it to death until it goes home to perdition and I go home to glory!"

Sunday was also an outspoken opponent of Major League Baseball scheduling games on the Lord's day. Due, in part, to his zealous campaign, several teams, including the Pirates, refused to play home games on Sundays.

# Chuck Tanner

Manager Chuck Tanner, who guided the Pirates from 1977-1985, had the honor of tying a record that will never be topped in any league. During his first major-league at-bat on April 12, 1955, as a pinch hitter for pitcher Warren Spahn, Tanner hit the first pitch from Cincinnati's Gerry Staley for a home run. As it turned out, this would be a career highlight for the young Milwaukee Braves outfielder. From 1955 to 1962, he would hit only 20 more homers. Even Warren Spahn would end his career after hitting 14 more home runs than Tanner.

Ironically, Tanner's "record" would be matched 15 years later by a rookie catcher with the Detroit Tigers, who would also become a Pirates manager from 1997-2000. Young Gene Lamont had shown so much promise that he was selected ahead of the great Johnny Bench in the 1965 amateur draft. However, that potential never materialized; Lamont ended his five-year career hitting a grand total of four homers.

# Pie Traynor

Many veteran fans who remember seeing Pie Traynor, Brooks Robinson, Clete Boyer and other great defensive third basemen claim that Traynor was, indeed, the greatest of all time. One sportswriter echoed their conclusion when he penned this accolade, "A batter hit a double down the left field line, and Traynor threw him out at first."

\* \* \*

Harold J. "Pie" Traynor came by his nickname when he was growing up in Sommerville, Massachusetts. When he was too young to play baseball on his parish team, he sat far behind home plate, shagged foul balls and brought them back to the field of play. Whenever the priest, Father Nangle, took him to the grocery store as a reward for his efforts, Traynor would say, "I'll take pie."

*Some veteran fans claim that Harold J. "Pie" Traynor was the greatest third baseman of all time.*

# Andy Van Slyke

One of the masters of satire in the world of sports was outfielder Andy Van Slyke, who played for the Bucs from 1987-1994. During the '92 season, when he was on a tear, hitting .324 with a league-leading 199 hits, he counseled a rookie who had received some bad press the night before. Van Slyke, no friend of sportswriters himself, said, "Ballplayers shouldn't gripe about reporters. A ballplayer should stay on a reporter's good side. Say nice things. Admire his clothes. Compliment him on his T-shirt."

\* \* \*

The 1988 Pirates introduced a roster of 25 fun-loving players who provided a lot of entertainment. They enjoyed themselves and played with a competitive spirit that endeared them to Pirates fans and media. Managed by Jim Leyland, the likes of Bobby Bonilla, Barry Bonds, Mike LaValliere and Doug Drabek clawed their way to a second-place finish behind the New York Mets.

Part of that feisty squad was Andy Van Slyke, who was acquired from St. Louis the year before. Van Slyke was a terrific addition to the ball club. His defensive skills sparkled that year as he led the National League by throwing out five runners. Van Slyke also enjoyed playing in Pittsburgh, especially having the

*Prankster Andy Van Slyke tries to assure manager
Jim Leyland that he will take the game seriously.*

opportunity to be part of a group of teammates who, unlike other
organizations, did not take themselves too seriously.

In comparing the Bucs with his former team, Van Slyke said,
"With the Cardinals, everybody in the clubhouse would be reading
the business section of the newspaper to see what their stocks were
doing. You go to our locker room in the morning, and everybody
is looking at the sports page to see if Hulk Hogan won his latest
match in the World Wrestling Federation."

# Arky Vaughan

Hall of Fame shortstop Joseph Floyd "Arky" Vaughan played the first 10 of his 14 major-league seasons with the Bucs. However, the Pirates would have lost the native of Clifty, Arkansas (the reason for his nickname), had it not been for the pragmatic wisdom of club owner Barney Dreyfuss.

In 1931, Vaughan was an infielder for Wichita, a Pirates farm team in the old Western League. A scout for the New York Yankees spotted the youngster and sent word to Yankees owner Jake Ruppert: "This kid from Arkansas is a 'sure thing.'"

Ruppert was impressed and eagerly wanted to buy the unproven minor-leaguer. He was so intent to add Vaughan to his stable that he sent a telegram to Mr. Dreyfuss in which he offered $40,000—a tidy sum of money in that era—for the rights to the youngster.

Dreyfuss, indeed, was tempted. That money could go a long way in helping to finance his struggling franchise.

Word of the offer reached the Pittsburgh media. Veteran reporter Chilly Doyle of the *Sun-Telegraph* asked Dreyfuss, "Barney, you're going to take the money, aren't you?"

Dreyfuss smiled and shook his head. "Nope," he said. "If the kid's worth that much to Ruppert, he must be worth as much to me."

*Arky Vaughan, an underrated shortstop, was a
mainstay in the Pirates' infield from 1932 to 1941.*

As it turned out, Dreyfuss was correct. Vaughan came to the
parent club the next year and hit .318. Three years later, he led
the league with a phenomenal .385 average. He would go on to
appear in nine All-Star Games and be inducted into Cooperstown
in 1985.

# Honus Wagner

Most baseball experts list John Peter "Honus" Wagner among the greatest shortstops of all time. When we consider that this Carnegie, Pennsylvania native spent 21 seasons in the big leagues with the old Louisville Colonels (the team that merged with the existing Pittsburgh club in 1900) and the Pirates, compiling a .327 average and leading the National League in batting eight times, it's no wonder that he is still regarded as one of the true giants of the game.

Because of his overwhelming statistics, a special committee appointed by baseball commissioner Kenesaw Mountain Landis elected to baseball immortality the first five inductees into the Hall of Fame. The players selected in 1936 were Babe Ruth, Ty Cobb, Christy Mathewson, Walter Johnson and the Pirates' own Honus Wagner.

Because the building at Cooperstown was not yet constructed, the official induction of the five pioneers did not take place until June 12, 1939.

\* \* \*

With his huge, muscular frame, the 5'11", 200-pound shortstop known as the "The Flying Dutchman" did not appear to be a threat on the base paths, especially when even the baggy baseball knickers worn by the players of the Dead Ball Era could not hide his pronounced bowed legs. However, Wagner led the National League five times in stolen bases, amassing a career total of 722—ninth on Major League Baseball's all-time list.

As Casey Stengel often said, "You can look it up."

\* \* \*

One of the retired numbers lining on the upper-deck facade at PNC Park is the "33" worn by Hall of Famer Honus Wagner. What might surprise many fans is that Wagner never wore that number when he played for the Pirates. In fact, nobody wore numbers by the time Wagner retired in 1917. The first players ever to wear numbers were the 1929 New York Yankees.

Why, then, is the number 33 retired in honor of Wagner? This is the number he wore when he was hired as a coach for the Bucs in 1933, a position he held with the club for 19 seasons.

As reported in Lawrence S. Ritter's *The Glory of Their Times*, Pirates great Paul Waner remembered that the aging coach would get out onto the diamond once in a while and take infield practice. "A hush would come over the whole ballpark, and every player on both teams would stand there like a bunch of little kids. I'll never forget it."

\* \* \*

Honus Wagner, as great a player as he was, never got to compete in the annual All-Star Game. The reason is simple. Wagner retired in 1917; the All-Star Game, a concept of *Chicago Tribune* sportswriter Arch Ward, was not played until 1933.

Wagner may be the oldest player ever to debut in the Midsummer Classic when, at age 70, he was named as a coach for the National League team in 1944—the year the game was first played at Forbes Field.

\* \* \*

*Honus Wagner shows former Pirate Frank Gustine Chief Wilson's bat in January of 1955.*

During the heyday of Honus Wagner when "The Flying Dutchman" was the most feared right-handed hitter in all of baseball, opposing pitchers tried to solve the riddle of how to pitch to the husky shortstop. During one contest with the New York Giants, Wagner approached the plate to lead off the inning, facing a rookie pitcher who had just entered the game. The pitcher stared at Wagner, then motioned for his manager, John McGraw, to join him on the mound. When a puzzled McGraw approached, the young hurler asked, "What shall I pitch to him?"

McGraw looked him squarely in the eye and said, "Just pitch anything—then duck." McGraw turned and walked back to the dugout, leaving behind a wide-eyed, stunned pitcher.

\* \* \*

"Nobody ever saw anything graceful or picturesque about Wagner on the diamond. His movements have been likened to the gambols of a caracoling elephant. He is ungainly and so bowlegged that when he runs, his limbs seem to be moving in a circle after the fashion of a propeller. But he can run like the wind."
—*New York American*, Nov. 19, 1907.

\* \* \*

Honus Wagner began a trend for Major League Baseball players who wished to earn a few dollars to supplement their incomes. In 1904, when players' salaries were such that even the so-called "superstars" (even though the term had not yet been used) had to get part-time jobs during the off season just to earn enough to make a living, Wagner was the first to be paid for endorsing a product. He allowed his name to be put onto a baseball bat.

Wagner, however, was extremely conscious of how his name was used. In 1909, Wagner had signed a contract for $10,000. While this may not be a whopping salary when compared with today's standards, in that era it made headline news. Therefore,

Wagner did not need money from endorsements to make ends meet. As a result, he could be more selective in authorizing companies to use his name.

The American Tobacco Company advertised in *The Sporting News* that a baseball card featuring Wagner's color photo would be included in selected packs of Piedmont, Sweet Corporal and Sovereign Cigarettes. Wagner protested. It wasn't because he disliked tobacco; he was a frequent smoker and chewer of a variety of brands. Wagner was concerned that a promotional stunt such as this might encourage young people to spend money for cigarettes. He demanded that the company cease and desist from this practice.

The company complied, but not until a handful of pictures were distributed.

Today, the actual number of cards remaining is debatable. Recently, a buyer from southern California outbid 12 others on eBay and bought one of those scarce cards known as the "Mona Lisa of Baseball Cards" or the "Holy Grail of Baseball Memorabilia" for an eye-popping $1.1 million, plus a buyer's premium of $165,000.

\* \* \*

Honus Wagner loved to spin yarns. To their dismay, after their columns appeared in the morning newspapers, many journalists discovered that the stories were, to put it kindly, results of Wagner's powerful imagination.

Some of his tales were easy to spot as "whoppers." One of Wagner's favorites was about the time he allegedly hit a baseball over the outfield fence in a sandlot game, and the baseball flew into the smoke stack of a passing steam locomotive. Before the ball could hit any surface, it was blown high into the air by the force of the steam and carried back over the fence into the waiting glove of the outfielder, thus turning a home run into an easy out.

Other tales were not so easy to discern. This author, in fact, was taken in by one of them.

When I was 15 years old, I had the opportunity to meet the famed Wagner at his house of worship—St. John's Lutheran Church in Carnegie. During our conversation, he described to several of us with explicit detail how, in Game 1 of the 1909 World Series against Ty Cobb and the Detroit Tigers, Cobb was on first base with no outs. As he was known to do, the infamous Cobb attempted to antagonize Wagner by shouting, "Hey, Krauthead! You better watch yourself, 'cause I'm coming down on the next pitch." Coming from Cobb, that was a threat. Cobb had already earned a reputation for sliding into second with his spikes high, causing anxieties for the fielder who had to avoid being hurt. Wagner told me how Cobb took off with the next pitch, but the catcher rifled a perfect throw to Wagner, who was covering the bag. Wagner caught the ball and swiped the ball and glove across the face of the sliding Cobb. In doing so, Wagner said that he knocked loose one of Cobb's teeth. The "Georgia Peach" suffered not only the humiliation of being smacked down by Wagner, but also of hearing the umpire yell: "Yer out!"

It's a great story, but totally untrue. Not only is it illogical that two such stars would chance getting into an altercation during a World Series, but the records clearly show that Cobb was never thrown out on an attempted steal during this game.

During this World Series, hyped as a match between Cobb and Wagner—the game's biggest superstars of the era—Wagner managed to out-perform Cobb in nearly every offensive department. He out-hit Cobb .333 to .231; he had six RBIs and six stolen bases, while Cobb had six RBIs and only two swiped bases.

And that's not just a "story."

\* \* \*

Those who knew him well agree that Honus Wagner, indeed, was a terrific storyteller—as long as his audience was limited to one or two. In front of a large crowd, however, he sometimes had problems stringing his words together. According to a report in the November 7, 1914, edition of *Sporting Life*, Wagner was in St. Joseph, Missouri, to attend a banquet in his honor. When

Wagner was invited to the podium, he looked out at the large crowd filling the banquet hall and, for a few seconds, said nary a word. Finally, following an awkward silence, "The Flying Dutchman" said, "Well... here I am, standing up to make a speech. But I don't know what I am going to say. Well, I can't see any use in standing here, so I guess I might just as well sit down."

He did just that.

# Dixie Walker

Fred R. "Dixie" Walker spent the last two years (1948-1949) of his major-league career playing outfield and an occasional first base with the Bucs. Because of his southern roots, he had a difficult time adjusting to the presence of Jackie Robinson while he was playing for the Brooklyn Dodgers. Consequently, Walker asked to be traded. One year later, general manager Branch Rickey agreed, and he sent Walker to the Pirates along with pitchers Hal Gregg and Vic Lombardi in exchange for Billy Cox, Gene Mauch and Elwin "Preacher" Roe. As it turned out, the trade worked well for both teams.

\* \* \*

"Dixie" Walker had earned another nickname while playing with the Dodgers. It was "The People's Cherce" (an emphasis of the local dialect known as "Brooklynese"). This origin of the nickname involved an ex-Pirate.

In 1941, an aging (38 years old) Paul Waner signed on with the Dodgers. Immediately after spring training, Dodgers manager Leo Durocher announced his intention to start Waner in right field in lieu of Walker—a fan favorite. When the Brooklyn faithful got wind of the decision, the Dodger front office was flooded with more than 5,000 protests.

*Sluggers Wally Westlake, "Dixie" Walker, Ralph Kiner and
Johnny Hopp gave the Pirates some hope during the 1948 campaign.*

Although Durocher did not waver from his choice, Walker eventually won back his starting role by hitting .311 and helped his club to win the National League pennant.

The was obvious that Walker had proven to the club's management and to the local media that he was indeed the "choice of the people."

# Lloyd Waner

Hall of Famer Lloyd "Little Poison" Waner, who started the 1941 season as a part-time outfielder for Pittsburgh and continued with two other teams that year, had 219 official at-bats. What is amazing is the fact that in this entire stretch, Waner did not strike out one time.

During each of his 18 years as a player in Major League Baseball, the younger of the two Waner brothers struck out as many as 20 times only twice, and in several years the number of "Ks" was below 10. In his recorded 7,772 official at-bats in the 1,993 games he played, Lloyd Waner struck out only 173 times. Compare this with Bobby Bonds of the San Francisco Giants, who struck out a record 189 times in just one season (1970).

*"Little Poison" and "Big Poison" try to determine just how many hits remain in their bats.*

# Paul Waner

Baseball players in the '30s and '40s were not the most sophisticated occupants of this planet. Most of them were farm boys or laborers who honed their baseball skills to earn money playing the game they loved. As a result, they played hard and, for the most part, drank hard.

One of the most heralded drinkers in all of baseball was Pirates headliner Paul Waner. Rumor had it that he was known to take a nip or two prior to a night game, and even between double headers. Waner later confessed that he often had to do 15 minutes of backflips to overcome hangovers before games.

While Waner may have spent a lot of time in local saloons, his extra-curricular activities with alcohol never affected his play. That fact was verified by William Lyman Hall, manager of a local Sealtest milk plant, who was a close friend of many of the Pirates players. "The best right fielder the Pirates ever had was Paul Waner when he was sober," Hall said. "The second best right fielder the Pirates ever had was Paul Waner when he was drunk."

\* \* \*

"Paul Waner had to be a graceful player, because he could slide without breaking the bottle in his hip pocket."
—Casey Stengel

* * *

Paul Waner and his brother Lloyd (both of whom were inducted into Baseball's Hall of Fame), were nicknamed "Big Poison" and "Little Poison." How they got these nicknames is debatable. While they were both the same size—5' 8 1/2"—Paul was a few pounds heavier and three years older than Lloyd. One story says that the opposing teams considered them "poison." A second claims that it started at Ebbets Field. As longtime newspaper man Red Smith explained, "*Poison* is Brooklynese for *person*. One Dodgers fan complained, 'Every time you look up those Waner boys are on base. It's always the little poison on thoid and the big poison on foist.'"

That fan may have not been far off in his analysis. The record books show that Lloyd Waner (a .316 lifetime average) and Paul Waner (a .333 lifetime average) compiled the highest batting average by siblings who played Major League Baseball.

Something that might come as a surprise to even the most sophisticated Pirates fan is that the player who holds the team record for runs batted in during a season is not Ralph Kiner, Willie Stargell, Roberto Clemente, or any of the other names that might come to mind. Instead, the record was set in 1927 when Paul Waner knocked in 131 runs. And he did this when hitting only nine home runs during the 154-game schedule.

# Bill Werle

Southpaw Bill Werle spent a bit more than three years (1949-1952) with the Pirates, primarily as a relief pitcher. In one particular game in Philadelphia during his rookie season, young Werle faced Bill "Swish" Nicholson—a long-ball hitter—with two men on base and two outs. When Nicholson took a hefty swing and popped the ball straight up into the air in front of the mound, Werle breathed a sigh of relief. As he was trained, Werle quickly called out the name of the fielder who should make the play.

"Eddie's got it! Eddie's got it!" he yelled.

Catcher Eddie Fitzgerald, third baseman Eddie Brockman and first-baseman Eddie Stevens stopped in their tracks and looked on helplessly as the ball fell untouched to the ground.

# Owen Wilson

John Owen "Chief" Wilson, an outfielder for the Pittsburgh
Pirates from 1908-1912, set a record that may be even more dif-
ficult to break than either Cal Ripken's 2,632 consecutive-game
streak or Joe DiMaggio's 56-game hitting streak. Nicknamed
"Chief" because he claimed his great grandfather was a Native
American, Wilson played all of his home games in spacious Forbes
Field. Because club owner Barney Dreyfuss hated the so-called
"cheap" home runs hit in other ballparks, he constructed the
Pirates' home park with plenty of room—360 feet down the left
field line, 376 feet to the right field foul pole and a whopping
462 feet to dead center. In 1912, Wilson took advantage of this
vast real estate to slam 36 triples.

That was nearly twice as many as were hit that year by his
nearest rivals, teammate Honus Wagner and the Giants' John
"Red" Murray, who each had 20.

Forbes Field became a haven for triples hitters. During its existence (1909-1970), the huge venue in Schenley Park allowed the
Pirates to finish a year with the most triples in a season 16 times.

In the "strange as it may seem" department, while Chief
Wilson hit 36 three-baggers in the 1912 season, during the other
eight years of his major-league career, he hit a grand total of only
78 triples.

# Jim Woods

From 1958-1969, Jim Woods was the number two man in the Pirates' broadcast booth with Bob Prince. Woods earned credentials as a sports reporter at KGLO in Mason City, Iowa, and waited for his big break. That came in 1937, when he was asked to replace the man who, for four years, had been the voice of University of Iowa football. The man Woods replaced was Ronald Wilson Reagan, who had left for Hollywood to pursue a career in acting.

As Jim Woods used to say, "Rumor has it that Reagan eventually went on to even bigger and better things."

\* \* \*

Bob Prince used to refer to Jim Woods as "Possum." That handle was given by New York Yankees ace pitcher and Hall of Famer Whitey Ford when Woods was an announcer for the Bronx Bombers prior to joining the Pirates. Ford claimed that Woods, with his close-cropped silver hair, resembled a possum. From that day on, he could not escape the nickname.

# Kevin Young

On August 30, 2002, representatives of the Major League
Baseball owners, the Players' Union, and the Office of the Baseball Commissioner met in New York City to hammer out a labor
agreement that would avert a strike, which could have threatened
not only the season, but the future of big-league baseball as we
know it.

Representing the Pirates players was popular first baseman
Kevin Young. Young was optimistic that the two sides would be
able to get together. When the threat of a strike ended just hours
prior to the start of the first game scheduled for that afternoon,
Young told reporters, "The fans of Pittsburgh will be a lot happier.
They have a beautiful ballpark and a talented team on the field
to compete, and have an opportunity to win the division, which
will mean more money for Downtown."

Those on the "inside" of baseball contend that the settlement of the disputes between labor and management in 2002
was made possible because of the cooperative attitude brought
to the bargaining table by representatives such as Kevin Young.

*First baseman Kevin Young helped keep baseball alive in 2002.*

BIBLIOGRAPHY

Bird, John T., *Twin Killing* (Birmingham, AL, Esmerelda press, 1995)

Dewey, Donald and Acocella, Nicholas, *The New Biographical History of Baseball* (Chicago: Triumph, 2002)

Fulton, Bob, *Pirates Treasures* (Pittsburgh: Goose Goslin, 1999)

Hageman, William, *Honus* (Champaign, IL, Sagamore Publishing, 1996)

Kerrane, Kevin, *Dollar Sign on the Muscle* (NY: Beaufort Books, 1984)

Kuenster, John, *Heartbreaks* (Chicago: Ivan R. Dee, 2001)

Leventhal, Josh, *The World Series* (NY: Black Dog & Leventhal, 2001)

Lieb, Frederick, *The Pittsburgh Pirates* (NY: G.P. Putnam's Sons, 1948)

McCollister, John, *The Best Baseball Games Ever Played* (NY: Citadel/Kensington Publishing, 2002)

McCollister, John, *The Bucs! The Story of the Pittsburgh Pirates* (KS: Addax Press, 1998)

O'Brien, Jim, *We Had 'Em All the Way* (Pittsburgh: Jim O'Brien, 1998)

Prime, Jim,' *Tales from the Red Sox Dugout* (Champaign, IL: Sports Publishing, 2001)

Shouler, Ken, *Book of Fabulous Facts & Awesome Trivia* (NY: Quill, 1999)